THE LAWGIVER

—AND—

OTHER POEMS.

BY MISS JANE ROSEBOOM.

"Let Fate do her worst: there are relics of Joy,
Bright beams of the past, which she cannot destroy;
And which come in the night-time of sorrow and care,
To bring back the features that Joy used to wear."

HILLSDALE, MICH.:
PUBLISHED BY THE AUTHOR.
1878.

W. S. GEORGE & CO.,
Printers and Binders,
LANSING, MICH.

DEDICATION.

TO THE MEMORY OF

MY LOVED MOTHER,

WHOSE SPIRIT LONG SINCE FOUND REST IN THE BETTER LAND,

AND WHOSE

TENDER CARE AND SYMPATHY ARE STILL CHERISHED IN MY HEART,

WITH ALL THE FULLNESS OF

THAT MOTHER'S LOVE CHEERING ME ONWARD

THIS LITTLE BOOK

IS MOST AFFECTIONATELY

DEDICATED.

CONTENTS.

PRELUDE.

To the natural eye, as we contemplate the vast field of Literature, we say, "Of books there is no end, yet the world is not full."

Enthusiasm, with its rising progress, well ever command its own on the calendar of reason.

My own little book, filled with sheaves which I have gathered from my own garner, owing to the edicts of an over-ruling Providence I offer to the public. I can see no reason for an apology. Hope has laid her corner-stone; whilst Faith, like a day-star, has guided me onward.

Results have their fastening in the dim future, and I can only do that which I believe to be right, even though I tremble before the mighty.

How I am to be judged, how I am to be spoken of, are matters to which I am truly sensitive; yet I cannot, for one moment, feel that there are those among you who would cast upon me a dark frown, or criticise with an eye too severe for endurance; though yours is the right to *criticise*, and mine to *bear* it.

THE LAWGIVER.

Beneath the welkin broad and blue,
And pure as heaven's unchanging hue,
The beams of morn and zephyrs mild
Caressed the river-floating child.
Like dew upon the flowers at dawn,
Or freshest verdure of the lawn,
So on his brow sat smiling grace,
And beauty gleamed upon his face.
By chance the ark upon the tide
The king's fair daughter soon espied,
And with a tender, anxious heart,
To bring it bade her maid depart.
And soon, impatient of delay,
They brought the little boat to bay,
Deep wondering what such casket kept.
A little child! Behold! it wept.

The maiden's love the babe embraced,
And on a mother's bosom placed;
Nor little thought she of the state
Existing 'tween the small and great.

As the deep waters smoothly glide,
Far from the torrent's angry tide,
So yields the will to destiny,
And maid and matron both agree.
A secret dearer far than gold,
That mother's joy, was left untold,
While fondly with her lips she pressed
The infant, folded to her breast.
Lo! Miriam's watch and wiser skill
Brought back the boon more lovely still;
A precious gem for Israel's brow,
To which both king and priest should bow.

When all his infant days were done,
And childhood's years had just begun,
The princess claimed again the boy:
The mother yielded up her joy,
But as a flower transplanted, there
On richer soil to bloom and bear,

With filial love his bright eyes beamed,
And wisdom from his visage gleamed.

They at proper age did place
The youth or of the kingly race,
At the Egyptian court, where he
Abode most eminent and free;
A life of rank and lustre lay,
As 'twere, athwart his sunlit way.
Perchance to him a kingly crown,
Glist'ning with glory and renown,
Should yet descend.

Hail, man of God!
Upon the fair, broad earth ne'er trod
One who could thus a throne forego,
A true pre-eminence to show.
His manhood brought him back to stay,
As he was wont, upon a day,
Among his brethren, kindred dear,
Who knew not of the tie so near.
But sudden ill did then provoke,
And on his inmost spirit broke.

A harsh Egyptian's cruel hand
Did smite one of the Hebrew band.
That fiendish act he clearly saw,—
A brother smitten without law.
It caused heroic zeal to burn;
He 'gainst the foe did madly turn;
Who then, for doing thus, was doomed,
Soon slew, and in the sand entombed.
Though hushed those deep and deadly blows,
Swift and appalling fear arose.
So madly had he loved his own,
This princely state was now a loan
To be repaid, that with a meek,
True soul, he Israel's good might seek.

Nor was he all alone; the ear
Of Majesty was drawing near.
He heard the groanings as they came
From His beloved; and he the same
Respect had then as e'er before
Their fathers he had shown of yore.
It came to pass that on a day
The exile with his flocks did stray

Far back into the desert space;
To man 'twere like a hiding place.
Lo! there a fiery flame upreared;
The angel of the Lord appeared,
And in a form most wondrous came,
For it was like a burning flame
From out the wayside bush, and so
The Infinite, in wondrous glow
Vouchsafed, not to intimidate,
But mingled so most intimate.
Then Moses turned him to the light,
That he might more behold the sight,—
A burning bush, yet unconsumed.
The Lord, who there in depths illumed,
Pronounced, in accents loud and clear
As ever mortal ear could hear,
A name. That name, how deep it fell
Upon his ear, no tongue can tell.
With trembling soul did he reply
To God Jehovah, "Here am I."
So trembling more he feared to look,
But still with painful tremor shook.
God spake, in one unaltered sound:
"The place thou tread'st is holy ground.

I've surely seen, my ear has heard,
My Hand Omnipotent is stirred;
And now I have come down to give
Deliverance, that they may live
Beyond the bidding of a host
Who make of cruelty a boast.
As high as heaven their groaning's plain,
Affliction, suffering, and pain.

"Behold thy father's God at hand;
My oath with Abraham shall stand.
For those for whom I long have cared
A home is even now prepared."
The great commission then he gave
To lead from Egypt every slave.
But Moses, filled with modest fear,
Cried, "Who am I? They will not hear."
He paused awhile, 'mid fear and dread,
But soon by miracles was fed.
The God, the friend of Abraham,
Plainly declared himself, "I Am;"
And by his marv'lous working skill,
Wrought demonstrations of his will.

The wondrous changing of the rod
Evinced the constancy of God.

The gen'rous hand that leads by might
Quells not the soul in darksome night,
But in drear hours He'll yet console,
Will strengthen, pity, and control.
So Moses by His hand was led,
As to the Egyptian court he sped;
And there besought at Pharaoh's hand
Permission to the desert land
To lead the Hebrews, there to bring
Before their God an offering.
The king replied, "Should I obey
His voice, and Israel go away?
I know him not, nor will I show
Assent, nor let the Hebrews go."

The ways of God are always wise;
In soundless depths His goodness lies.
His knowledge taught a better way
Than princely skill could e'er essay.
He prompted well His people's heart,
And pledged from them He'd not depart;

But would on Egypt lay his hand,
To prove the living God's command.
Then Moses strove with Pharaoh long,
And urged with kindly pleadings strong;
But he by turns still harder grew,
After each plague so strange and new,
Till, overwhelmed in sorrow's night,
All Egypt cried for Israel's flight.

"Go, get you forth, ye people all,
Ye young and old, both great and small;
And all your flocks and herds away.
Within these bounds no longer stay,
But to the desert region go,
To serve your God as best you know."
They, with a willing, longing heart,
Prepared with swiftness to depart.
Their leader, Moses, they obeyed,
And from the Egyptian land they strayed.
Round through the wilderness they trod
The way, as spoken of by God.
The pillar of a cloud by day
Disclosed through pathless wilds the way;

And in the darksome hours of night
A fiery pillar gave them light.
But when they saw the host pursue,
And nearer, closer, Pharaoh drew,
They deemed it had been best to stay,
Proud Egypt's king to serve alway.
Spake Moses to the multitude,
And back their waning courage wooed:
"Stand still, and fear you not; I say
Salvation shall be shown to-day;
For the Egyptians whom ye see,
With them ye never more shall be.
So hold your peace; it shall be true,
The Lord of Hosts will fight for you."

According to the word of God,
As verified, he took the rod,
And with an outstretched arm swayed o'er
The deep, where angry surges roar.
The wind blew up, the deep fell back,
And left a dry and sandy track.
On which the people hasted through,
Eager their journey to pursue.

On right and left a watery wall;
Behind, the pillar veiled them all.
Still Pharaoh thought to follow, too,
And dared with chariots to pursue
Down 'midst the billowy deep profound,
Where he and all his hosts were drowned;
And thus it was by judgment shown
That Israel's God was Lord alone.

THE SONG OF MOSES.

My trust is in the living Lord,
  And He my strength shall be;
Exalt His name, let words of praise
  Arise, from Israel free.

The triumph is most glorious,
  Thy foes are overthrown;
The sea has covered each of them,
  Whilst light to us is shown.

The chariots strong, and hosts so great,
  Are buried in the sea;
Yea, too, the lordly ones are lost
  By their audacity.

Thy outstretched arm and mighty hand
  O'erthrew those who arose;
Whom with thy blast did'st thou consume,
  And their injustice close.

With thine Almighty breath thou mad'st
  The waters stand on heap;
So stood the floods as if congealed,
  Like walls, the watery deep.

The enemy with wild delight
  Still said: I will pursue;
My hand, my sword, shall yet destroy,
  Your flight ye soon shall rue.

Thou bad'st the wind, the sea return,
  They sank as lead within;
So fell the host of rebels, fraught
  With harsh inhuman sin.

But Thine own chosen ones of yore,
  On whom Thine eye was set,
Are safely now on freedom's soil,
  To prove thy goodness yet.

It was a proud, a happy day,
When each broke forth in joyous lay.
A victory now they all could boast,
For low were laid the Egyptian host.
No heart could boast its valor then,
The Lord of Hosts had fought for men.
Ere they could reach the promised ground,
Long, toilsome years must roll around;
They journey on from place to place,
O'er cragged hills, or barren space,
With two, uniting hand in hand,
Beloved of God, in friendship's band,
Who stood as chief 'mid friend or foe,
Wherever they should stay or go.
God called them forth, His voice obeyed,
Anon their weary footsteps stayed.

So quick and sensitive the ear,
That never lists in vain to hear,
And never fails the truth to know,
God caught the murmur deep and low,
That spoke the shameful doubt and fear
Of those he loved and cherished dear.
With all His gen'rous hand had done,
And all the glorious victory won,
They feared to trust Him for their bread,
But raised a murm'ring voice instead.
Oh! frail and erring ones, to chide
Your only earthly hope and guide!
Who lent the cloud to lead by day
Through all the wilderness the way,
A fiery pillar all the night
To lead you through the wilds aright;
And, when shut up before the sea,
A pathway through it made for thee!
Then think you He would fail to feed,
Or keep you in the hour of need?

But Israel sinned, yet were not they
From gift of mercy cast away.

Jehovah stooped, with love profound,
And strewed the manna on the ground.
With grateful hearts they ate their fill,
But when athirst they murmured still,
And tempted God, who faithful is,
O'er the long cherished flock of His.
Unstable man! how doubts arise,
When blessings once escape the eyes.
Has faith to stay thy soul no power,
No charm to break the darksome hour?

But he, the leader of the band,
Who swayed the host by his command,
Relying on the God he knew,
From Him his inspiration drew,
And for the millions in his care,
Would raise a supplicating prayer.
And so, to him a thirsty spot,
Where springs and living streams were not,
Could but disclose majestic skill,
And show his sovereign power to will.
As when, with rod in hand to knock,
He smote the hard and rugged rock,

The smitten rock gave way in part,
And let the hidden fountain start.
What fancied picture could portray
The depth of happiness that day?
No part of dark oblivion's night
Can quell the soul when led aright.
No battle group, no fiendish arm,
Can yield a pretext of alarm.
When war by Amalek was sent,
Above to pray the prophet went,
To take the rod of God in hand,
And there upon the hill to stand.
And then, with hand uplifted high,
He saw the sons of Israel vie
So vig'rously they were not long
Discomfiting the hostile throng.

No matter where thy path may be,
Some blissful buds will bloom for thee;
Some gentle heart will own thy smile,
With claims reciprocal the while.
And was it not a blissful scene
To find communion so serene,

In those drear wilds, with dearest ones,—
His wife, her sire, her darling sons
Whom he had borne upon his knee?
'Twas joy that angels bent to see.

They talked of what the Lord had done,
What glorious victories He had won,
Which heart-felt gratitude did wake,
As this was all for Israel's sake.
Thus Jethro's mind was deeply stirred,
Who uttered many a kindly word,
And, as a father to his son,
Advised what there were better done.
And Moses heard as Jethro spake,
And did from many burdens break.
In union sweet their hearts were one,
O'er all the many acts thus done.
Then, called again apart to dwell,
Each kindly uttered his farewell.

Then to the people Moses turned,
Whilst deep enthusiasm burned;
They move, and on to Horeb press,
To them an unknown wilderness,

Until at length the sight obtained,
The mount of Sinai they had gained,—
That sacred, consecrated height,
Whereon was known Jehovah's might.
In sight of all the people near,
That each might honor, love, and fear
The blest and holy one of God,
Who dwelt beneath his smile and nod,
God called him up the sacred hill,
To take the record of his will.
How vast the work for mortal man!
Of such a host to lead the van,
Approach to God with reverent awe,
And take from Him his holy law,—
Specific precepts plainly given,
To guide them on and up to heaven;
To guide them, too, while journeying here,
And hold them back from evils drear.
But who the wonderings could tell
Which even there on Israel fell?
His glory on the mountain's height
Was like a flame of dazzling light,

His thunder trump the earth did shake,
Making the stoutest fear and quake.

The cloudy vestment still abode;
Full well on Sinai's brow it showed;
And with the Lord upon its heights
He tarried forty days and nights.
The written law, on tablets strong,
Was given him to teach the throng;
And all the works and patterns too
Were even shown him how to do.
The cherub ark and mercy-seat,
With measured length and breadth as meet,
To be constructed all with grace,
His testimony there to place.

But ere he left the blissful seat
Where God he face to face did meet,
Jehovah said, "Go! I have known
Thy kin rebellious; all have shown
Themselves corrupt and very bold;
Have served an idol-god of gold.
Now let alone and stay me not,
My wrath against them shall wax hot;

These I'll consume whom thou hast led;
A nation make of thee instead."
But Moses mercy still besought
For Israel, whom his love had brought,
With outstretched arm and mighty hand,
From the oppressive, bitter land.
God lent to him an ear that day,
And from the evil turned away.

He then descended, took his stand,
With the two tables in his hand,
Which on them bore the written word,
Inscribed as never ear had heard,
Done by the hand of God alone,
Those table-written works of stone.
But soon, as near the camp he drew,
The molten idol-god to view,
His anger rose, one glimpse to take,
So much that he the tables brake.
Nor did his righteous ire subside
Until he'd thrown the god aside.
He burnt it and to powder ground,
Till nothing save the dust was found;

That, strewed he on the water's brink,
And of it made the people drink.

To Aaron, then, in grief turned he:
"What did this people unto thee,
That thou has brought them so to shame,
With wrath against them all aflame?"
"Let not the anger of my lord
Wax hot," replied he in a word.
"Thou knowest those thou seest to-day,
A very wicked people they.
'Make us a god,' they urgent said,
'One unto whom our hearts can wed;
For, as for Moses, once so bold,
Him we may never more behold.'
Whoever hath—thus spake I then—
A bit of gold, break off; and when
They did, I in the fire it threw,
And lo! this molten calf it grew."
Lord, what is man, that he'd devise,
And let such vain excuse arise?
Did not thy strength and wisdom shine,
Most wondrous, infinite, divine?

Those on God's side received the word,
Swift on them then the sword to gird,
The foul rebellion quick to quell:
'T was done, and there three thousand fell.
Then to the remnant did he say,
"Now consecrate yourselves to-day."
Then to Jehovah bent his way,
To pray, as humble suppliants pray,
Him from his book that God would blot,
If he could then forgive them not.
Jehovah said, "Who sin hath done
Against me, I'll blot out that one.
Now, therefore, lead the people through
To that bright land I've promised you.
Mine angel shall before you go,
A pathway through the wilds to show.
Their sin I'll visit on them still,—
This is my firm unchanging will.
I will requite; a plague shall stay
Upon the people many a day.

"Depart, I say, and go! Command
Those rescued from the Egyptian land

To seek the place I did prepare;
It flows with milk and honey there.
My presence still shall with you go,
And rest unto you I will show."
But Moses adds, with ardent mind,
Submissive, generous, and kind,
"Unless I share Thy presence thence,
I ask Thee, carry us not hence.
And now, O Lord, if in thy sight,
Who dost in mercy still delight,
I have found grace Thyself to know,
To me, I pray, thy glory show."
He asked, and lo! God passed before,
Proclaiming all his goodness o'er.

What kindness does He ever show,
Beyond what human creatures know.
He leaves no vacancies to fill,
Naught to subvert His glorious will.
Then spake He, "Hew two tables more;
I'll write thereon as writ before,
That Israel still may know my law,
And learn with rev'rent awe."

And Moses, with obedient hand,
Submissive to his Lord's command,
Prepared the tables all anew;
The Lord, all-merciful and true,
Re-wrote the covenant with care,
And each of the commandments there.
Down from the mount went Moses then,
To bear to man God's law again;
While all were awed by power divine,
Which made the bearer's face to shine.

As given him upon the mount,
So he to Israel did recount
The form as fashioned by each mark,
The cherubs, furniture, and ark.
And men, wise-hearted men, were there,
Their part in labor each to bear,
And work in art of grandest mould,
And overlay with shining gold,
Until the ark and mercy-seat
With cherubim were all complete.
Down to the smallest pattern shown,
That God the copy true might own.

They to the goodly work adhered
Till they the tabernacle reared.
Eeach did his work as it should be;
As was commanded, "So did he."

Then earthward from the golden height
Came radiant beams of glory bright,
Transcendent with a matchless hue,
And filled the tabernacle too.
Jehovah's goodness brooded o'er,
And blessed them still as oft before.
The fav'ring cloud that, day by day,
Should with the tabernacle stay,
Should be as fire unto the sight
Of Israel through the hours of night.
And when he wished them to pursue
Their onward journey, it updrew,
And when they saw it hov'ring close,
They journeyed not till it arose.

To Canaan's fair and fertile ground
Were all the host of Israel bound;
Unto that free and goodly soil,
Away from sorrow and turmoil,

With him whom God knew face to face,
With gifts of glory and of grace,
To lead them on, and teach them, too,
His hallowed ways so kind and true.
And well he bore the servant's part,
In pure fidelity of heart.

But oh! how sad their wand'rings were,
So soon again such murm'rings stir.
Against Jehovah, Lord of love,
With all His watch-care from above,
They did complain, nor would perceive
The way of justice, and believe.
So threats of vengeance did resound
Through fiery indignation round;
Yet could they no excuse afford,
For they by miracle and word
Were fed and cherished day by day,
To strengthen them upon the way.
But to their leader did they look,
And he himself to prayer betook.

How oft again the people durst,
With all the written word rehearsed,

Complain and chide that they were led
From Egypt, and on manna fed.
Alas! how many thousands fell
Of Israel's hosts who did rebel.

And when the messenger's were sent
(To spy the goodly land they went),
They brought such tidings, deep and sore,
As made all Israel weep the more,
And wish in Egypt they had died,
And all the plans of God deride,
Save Joshua and Caleb strong,
Who strove to quell the direful wrong;
Whilst deeply did their feelings burn
To think injustice should return.
For, 't is a goodly land, said they;
And if you'll not 'gainst God array,
Then he will still in us delight,
And those from Canaan's land will fright.

Then in His wrath, Jehovah spake,
"Herein your wasting-place I'll make.
The land concerning which I swore,
Not one full-grown shall reach its shore,

Except Jephunneh's faithful son,
And Joshua, the son of Nun."

What were the feelings that arose,
To see so many lost of those
Who, long upheld, should most adore
And reverence the God of yore!
But still in faith the leader's eye
Went beaming forward, thus to try,
According as God gave him grace,
To fill his sphere in every place.
The Hebrew host he guided on,
Till they at length were found upon
The plains of Moab, near the stream
Whose swelling billows brightly gleam,
And dash its waters far and wide
'Gainst the fair banks of Canaan's side.
The long, long pilgrimage was o'er;
They now should plod the waste no more,
But enter and possess the place
Promised so long before, and chase
With their invincible array
Each curs'd inhabitant away.

Yea, they were then upon the strand;
But he, who through the desert land
Had led them on, could ne'er attain,
Nor plant his foot upon the plain.
His one misdoing when in Zin
Deprived him of his entrance in.
Yet his integrity so bold
Was never otherwise than told.
The self-same pure and vivid will
That marked his character, was still.
His forty years' sojourn within
The wilderness more drear by sin
Was ended, and he must select
One who should in his stead direct.
To Joshua he gave command,
And upon him he laid his hand:
A man in whom the Spirit dwelt,
Who zeal for Israel had felt,
And now, as fitted well his name,
The leader of the host became.

The venerable servant left
The congregation not bereft

Of strength and wisdom to dispose;
And kind encouragements arose.
He'd seen the wonders of the Lord
Most marvelously shown toward
His people Israel at the sea,
Their triumph, glorious and free.
The march he now, in thought, renewed,
How he the desert path pursued,
And guided them so many years,
'Mid all their conflicts and their fears;
And how that solemn hour he spent
With Aaron, as appointed—went
Upon Mount Hor, where he should die—
The scene fled like a torrent by.
The fall of many, and the hour
Of justice and delivering power,
Swept o'er his mind, as mem'ry's eye
Reviewed the scenes that had gone by.

And to the people gathered near,
So that all Israel could hear,
He spake, and to their minds conveyed
Anew the laws to be obeyed:

"It is not a vain thing for you,
That these commands ye keep and do;
If thus ye enter to possess
The goodly land, He then will bless.
Full six score years are mine this day
And I remember God did say,
'Thou shalt not o'er this Jordan go.'
But Joshua the way shall show;
So heed with diligence his word,
And all the precepts ye have heard."

And as the time had well drawn nigh
In which he knew that he must die,
The little while he yet abode,
His heart poured forth in lofty ode,
And blessings full of tender care,
For the twelve tribes of Israel there.
The latest moment came; they took
With sorrowing hearts their last, last look.
His song had ceased, his prayers were made;
He turned away and gently bade
His last farewell to Israel.

His years and labors no inroad
Upon his energies yet showed;
And with his natural eye undim
He strode away from Jordan's brim,
And up the mount where he could view
From Pisgah top the vision new.
The land of Canaan, and the scene,
Wide-spread, expansive, and serene,
With thankfulness his heart did fill.
His eyes surveyed it long, until
'T was satisfied, then golden rays
Of glory broke on his full gaze,
Like angel beckonings from afar,
With the eternal gates ajar.
His great Creator thus he spied,
And bowed his drooping head, and died.

THE CRUCIFIXION.

How hurls thee back, O mind and will,
To that dark age of fiendish skill,
When man, vile man, with sinful hate,
Condemned and slew Messiah great.
I fancy I can see him 'most,
As when, before the lordly host,
So mildly meek, so fairly formed,
So beautiful, yet not adorned,
He stood before a common bar,—
Methinks the outer gate ajar,—
Accused amid an angry crowd,
Whose envious voices thundered loud.
But ah! no change their wak'nings stirred,
He list, but answered not a word.
The sentence came; but what was He,
That He should bear such enmity?

Be chastened, scourged, and spit upon,
His head with crown of thorns thereon?
Those cruel mockings, oh! how sore,
Such as were never known before.
Between two thieves be crucified,
Those hurtful felons madly cried.
Extreme beyond all other woe,
But cruelties such would not forego.

O kingly governor and host,
Why heed'st the bitter language most?
Own erring self too meekly led,
So from your lips the wild ire spread.
I scarce would thought that one of pride,
Who did not feel to coincide,
Could e'er have yielded to the plan,
And sentenced thus a spotless man.
But human art when basely played
Has for its toy a dark hour made.
And who with hideous wills condense
Should share alike the consequence.

I follow, on my mind's eye gaze
Far back into the olden maze;

And through the vista, calm and clear,
As lies through time's remotest year,
Those awful truths, beyong control,
Rush back into my inmost soul.
That day, that hour, but yet the word
Warm from his loving heart was heard:
"Weep not for me, but for self's own;
Weep for your children and bemoan,"
Seemed though 'twere spoken to allay
The horror of the dreadful day.
Yet doubtless His foreseeing eye
Was fixed on the destruction nigh.
Affection knows a charm, to bind
The tendrils of the heart entwined;
And when diffused with power and skill,
Will renovate th' unstabled will.
Such ignominious death to die,
The heavy cross before Him lie,
And more than that at first must bear,
So would with all the suffering share.
But when too weary, worn, and weak,
Another was compelled to seek;
On Simon lay the heavy load,
To trudge the tedious, tiresome road.

When down below, outside the wall,
Was mixed the vinegar and gall,
He took, indeed, the bitter cup,
But would not drink the portion up,—
Would rather stand alone in fate
Than use the stilling opiate.

Among the gathered multitude
Were many friends His love had wooed,
Who wept, would bitterly bewail;
But sympathy could not avail.
The vicious and the rude, to gain
The power, could 'chieve the deadly aim;
So, at Golgotha's loathsome spot,
They railed, but still He rallied not,
And would most viciously propose,
Regardless of the wills or woes.
'T was there the frightful scene began,
Among the base, uncomely clan,
Who were so ready to agree,—
They nailed Him to the cursed tree.

But hear what zeal did yet remain,
With all His weight of suffering pain,

Should utter ere in silence broke,
And for the enemy invoke:
"Father, forgive them, for they know not
What they do." Would fain have all forgot,
So willing and so kind was He,
Still loved with all His energy.
Fast weak'ning down, the spark expired;
He then from mortal toil retired.

How strangely sad to have appear,
And every soul be struck with fear,
Who had so little while before
Felt man-like, or as conquerors more.
But He, the ruling One on high,
Bespoke, and clouds betook the sky.
The golden sun at once was veiled;
With anger stirred, His wrath assailed
And shook and quaked with fearful might
The earth and rugged rocks aright.
And, too, the temple veil in twain
Was rent by this convulsive strain.
Absorbing, oh! where were the men
Who rallied so revengeful then?

As shrubs, without a leaf of green,
Left stalky, barren, or unclean,
They, one by one, abased and low,
Had felt the terror-striking blow.
The saw disclosed the sainted dead,
The shaken earth, the chasms spread;
The clouds obstructed from their sight
The golden rays of morning light;
Resistless, torpid, faint with fear,
Were conscience-smitten,—hope was drear,
For He, the ruling One on high,
Had brought the wreck of ruin nigh,
To testify Christ, King of host,
And prove him to the uttermost.
And well the Centurion meekly said,
When looking on the cold and dead,
In mid air, with a trembling nod,
"This truly was the Son of God."

THE GEHENNA OF FIRE.

THE GEHENNA OF FIRE refers to the dreadful punishment of being burnt alive in the Valley of Ben Hinnom, a valley on the southeast of Jerusalem, in which the idolatrous Jews sacrificed their children by fire to Moloch, Baal, and the sun. In one spot, called Tophet, was a fire-stone in which idolaters and other culprits were occasionally burnt. In it Josiah ordered all the offal, bones, carcasses of dogs and animals, and other filth, to be consumed; and to prevent the evil that might result from putrefaction and worms, the fire was never allowed to go out, but was kept incessantly burning, and thus it was a very fit and striking emblem of the everlasting fire of hell.

OH! that sad and mournful valley,
  Darkness hovered o'er the glen,
Though the light of fire blazing,
  And the Orient beams, were then
Spreading wide their brilliant vestment,
  Shadowing with a golden hue,

Lending rays of lusty clearness,
  Lovely as the crystal dew.
But there, 'midst the glow of nature,
  Earth's fair hills and valleys clad,
Bush and shrub, their beauty bearing,
  As to make the creature glad,
Cruel depths of heathen darkness
  Coiled the consciousness of soul;
Wrought a shade of deepest horror,
  E'er on memory could enroll.
Yes, those wild, deluded people,
  Stringent in their courses run,
Sacrificed their offerings to
  Moloch, Baal, and the sun.
Idol gods, as gods to worship,
  Worse than nothingness below.
Earth seemed made a solemn gateway
  To the one to which we go.
Minds to bear the hideous torture,
  Flesh and bones to ashes burn,
Who could think, in human likeness,
  Aught but would such sorrow spurn?

Mothers lay their infant children
  On those heated arms to fry;
Nursling infants, goodly offspring,
  Born for such a death to die!
Fathers, with sarcastic courage,
  Act the strange and vile device,
Heaping up abominations,
  Give their sons, a sacrifice.

Oh! that sad, that mournful valley,
  Where the dark of minds were led,
With a stony heart of hardness,
  Rankle round the suff'ring dead.
Wasting, ever wasting carcass,
  Human and inhuman both,
Burning constant, ever burning,
  Not such fumes of fire they loathe.
Could beneath the vault of heaven
  Ever such an emblem been,
As the fire of hell eternal,
  Built among the sons of men?

Thus it seems: but God of justice
  Thundered with majestic sway,
Called no more the valley Hinnom,
  Turned the miniature away.
God of earth, and God of nations,
  Wrecked and spoiled the wild delight,—
Showed himself the Maker, Ruler,
  In this world of day and night.

7

TO-DAY.

"A MAN'S life is a tower, with a stair-case of many steps,
That, as he toileth upward, crumble successively behind him;
No going back, the past is an abyss; no stopping, for the present perisheth;
But ever hastening on, precarious on the foothold of to-day.
Our cares all To-day, our joys are all To-day,
And in one little word, our life, what is it but To-day?"

—TUPPER.

COMPARE philosophers and wise,
Elate with wond'rous wisdom rise;
Compare by knowledge, power more true,
If can, than that the poet drew:
For what is life, but like a tower?
It upward tends from hour to hour.

We cannot pause, with eager flight,
We haste to see the coming plight,
And as we pass with deep regret,
So soon, alas! too soon, forget;

Forgotton time, with rapture wrung,
Into a dark abyss is flung.

Then should we care? It cannot be
That ever mortal eye can see
Or measure out the myriads past,
That in the dark abyss is cast;
But God's remembering book will tell
The annals of our history well.

And can we bring the cunning light
Of morning's unknown scenes to sight?
Ah, no! they're hid from day to day;
Will be, is all that we can say.
A long-swung shadowy veil is run,
Between to-day and to-morrow's sun.

The present, then, like a fluttering wing,
Our every care and our joy doth bring,
For life like a coming day may dawn,
And twilight have the requiem drawn.
Hallow in sacred awe, I say,
The precarious foothold of to-day.

Yet, ever hastening onward, toil
'Till we throw off this mortal coil.
To die, to live in peace arraigned,
Or live, to die in woe unfeigned.
Whatever then, whate'er so gay,
Our life, what is it but to-day?

SEPULCHRE;

OR, DEPOSIT FOR MAN AFTER DEATH.

"Thou shalt lie down
With patriarchs of the infant world, with kings,
The powerful of the earth, the wise, the good,
Fair forms, and hoary seers of ages past,
All in one mighty sepulchre."

—Bryant.

The mighty sepulchre, how great!
Deposit, too, for those of state;
Kings, from their high and lofty throne,
Do claim it for their secret home.

The powerful shall yield their head,
And rest in silence with the dead.
The earth contains the weak, the strong,
The wise, the good, in silence long.

Dust mingles with the dust again,
These comely forms shall not remain,
But, with the patriarchs of old,
Consign our bodies to the mould.

The mighty sepulchre, how great!
Oh! when shall' meet the dismal fate?
We know not when, nor will we know,—
The guiding hand does not foreshow.

But this we know, that all must die,
In secret silence all must lie.
The earth shall be our resting place
When we have run this weary race.

TRUST IN SUPREME RELIABILITY.

> "THOU go not like the quarry slave at night
> Scourged to his dungeon; but sustained and soothed
> By an unfaltering trust."
>
> —BRYANT.

How great that trust, supremely so,
When to the sepulchre we go;
Pillars our spirits, prompts us free,
For that more genial clime to see.

How great the doom—some think it great—
That we must leave this mortal state,
And enter in the nightly shade
Where all the ancient hosts are laid.

Why should you fear, you earth-bound crew?
The mighty sepulchre is for you.
Why should you shrink when He invites?
'T is but the bidding to delights.

You go not like the quarry slave,
Scourged to his dark and lonely cave;
But moved with majesty sublime,
And freed from all the tilts of time.

Do think again. Did not the hand
That leads you through this lower land
Dismount from yonder lofty place,
And travel through this dreary space?

Did He not leave a staff for thee,—
His loving spirit? Oh, how free!
It will sustain our parting breath,
And soothe us in the hour of death.

SECURITY.

> "Approach thy grave
> Like one who wraps the drapery of his couch
> About him, and lies down to pleasant dreams."
>
> —BRYANT.

The monarch, royalist, the brave,
The weak, the small, or stately grave,
Alike to all the darksome hall,
That cavern deep with shroud and pall.

Dim midnight, with its dusky air,
Can throw no shadows of despair
O'er dreamless slumbers, quiet breath,
When hushed in the embrace of death.

Then quietly your grave approach,
For no intruder can encroach,

Since Christ, the Sovereign One of God,
Has stayed the theft, and broke the clod.

All peacefully, with armor by,
Approach your humble grave, to lie
As one who takes his drapery vest
And wraps it 'bout to take his rest.

All pleasantly, with cheerful air,
A farewell day to toil and care,
As if—but ah! no dreams can tell,
All cordial, but no anthems swell.

A safe retreat from mortal woe,
A thoroughfare from things below,
A transport to the furth'rmost edge,
An exile from our pilgrimage.

Though deep the grave, a dismal pit,
'T will never be by wild-fires lit,
For there the myriads sleep when led,
Until archangels wake the dead.

FIGURE OF THE SUFFERING OF DEATH.

"**DEATH, subtile leech, hath anatomized soul from body,
Dissecting well in every nerve it split from its substance."**
—**TUPPER.**

DEATH, subtle leech, how deep entrenched,
When that of soul from substance wrenched.
What deep'ning shade, what fearful pain,
Must actuate when cleft in twain.

But gone, frail figure, sunken 'neath
The cold earth's breast their forms enwreath;
Death, frigid lord, has claimed his clay,
And Death, foul despot, seized his prey.

Not one, nor few, but all must share,
And meet grim Death, the tyrant, where
Or when he please,—we can't direct,
Or change the current to effect.

'Twas so ordained, but yet when I
Consider what it is to die,
It seems like such a rending break
The spirit from its substance take.

Ah me! who would not wish to serve?
Think of dissecting every nerve;
Those pangs so great, who would suggest,—
I own could never yet express.

But I am weak, frail one of earth,
My most is of but little worth;
My strength is in my Maker, God,
Who rules the nations with a rod.

'Twas His decree that man should die
To earth, and in its bosom lie;
However, to His will I'll bend,
And ever on His arm depend.

He heeds me, yea, frail nature heed,
Upmounted, yet He stoops to lead;
His throne on high o'er this domain,—
On earth, in heaven, alike to reign.

THE SPIRIT RETURNS TO GOD.

"Then shall the dust return to the earth as it was, and the spirit shall return to God who gave it."—BIBLE.

WHEN looking through the book of yore,—
That noted book of long before,—
I find recorded most sublime,
Pure words of truth in every line.

On death alone we need not dwell,
Or picture scenes for tongue to tell.
Though dust return to dust again,
Th' undying soul still lives to reign.

But not with elements below,
Here ling'ring round 'mid friend and foe,
As if to fear a princely tread,
O'er the cold relic,—sleeping dead.

But with the living God to bring,
Away our tired spirits wing;
To other home, another scene,
Of endless woe or bliss serene.

God gave a gift, and giving, bought,
And buying, asketh love should aught
Subdue, but live in faith and love
To join seraphic joys above.

Thou great, thou universal all,
Who died and conquered to recall,
For loan He left to hallowed bliss.
What more could any ask than this?

But be it with us as it may,
This flesh must mix with kindred clay;
And God our spirits will ensure,
And those are His, with Him secure.

DESTINY OF THE WICKED.

"DEPART from me, ye cursed, into everlasting fire, prepared for the devil and his angels."—BIBLE.

How will it seem to hear that sound
Pronounced to many millions round:
Depart from me, ye cursed, into
The gulf prepared, though not for you?

Then down the precipice below,
They down, down, deeper, further go,
Still cursing God, the Lamb, and scorn
The earth, the resurrection morn.

They'll seek for death, but vainly seek,
Yes, utter death would gladly meet;
But privileged scenes of time must mourn,
The final destiny be borne.

The fury of His vengeance now
Is fixed on every form and brow;
Must bear, be borne through ages bound,
An everlasting, changeless round.

A painful death that never dies,
A horrid gloom with bitter cries,
In fiery flames to ever be
Throughout a long eternity.

Dark night of agony and tears,
A night of days, and months, and years;
Still onward, onward, midst the gush
Of sorrow's agonizing crush.

Such is the harvest sin has sown;
Such harvest who'd not blush to own?
To dwell forever 'neath the rod
For trampling on the Son of God.

His means of grace, his mercy sure,
Could all a privilege secure.
But if they will, at last shall dwell
Forever in a dreadful hell.

DESTINY OF THE RIGHTEOUS.

"Come, ye blessed of my Father, inherit the kingdom prepared for you from the foundation of the world."

—Bible.

Now come, ye of my Father bless'd,
Inherit, take your sainted rest.
The kingdom was prepared for you,
And its effulgent glories, to.

How bless'd the sons of Adam's race,
Inherit such a dwelling-place.
So early, too, prepared for man,—
Must been prepared when time began.

Let's stop and think: what can this be,
This heavenly kingdom made for thee,
By Jove and Judge divinely wrought,
Love's great eternal centre fraught?

Jerusalem, that glorious home,
From where no blissful subjects roam;
Where the angelic hosts have trod,—
The glorious city of our God.

He framed the wall, so great and high,
With love-lit beams, like summer sky;
The streets He paved with shining gold,
Transparent as clear glass, we're told.

Foundation so most precious, too,
He built it all entirely new;
With jasper, sapphire, emerald grade,
For the adorning stones, were laid.

Those pearly gates, what price could count?
Each gate a pearl,—what could surmount
Such beauty and such grandeur sought?
Beyond our view His hand hath wrought.

That matchless worth, that heavenly place,
Where golden beams did darkness chase;
No nights are there, no pain or death,
But glory crowns the immortal breath.

Most blessed son of Adam's race,
Inherit such a dwelling-place;
Emmanuel's home, where angels meet,
And sing His praise majestic sweet.

A kingdom exquisitely fair,
And the redeemed have welcome there;
The ransomed ones have gained their rest,
For said He not, "Come ye, my bless'd?"

Life's glittering crown is on His brow,
And thus on all He places now,
And gladly welcomes round the throne,
As the good sheep the Shepherd own.

Most sweetly fell upon the ear,
In accents so divinely clear:
"Now come, ye of my Father bless'd,
Inherit, take your sainted rest.

"This kingdom was prepared for you,
And its effulgent glories too;
Each crown your own, with scepter stand,
Forever more at my right hand."

UNSEEN GLORIES OF THE HEAVENLY WORLD.

"**EYE hath not seen, nor ear heard, neither have entered into the heart of man, the things which God hath prepared for them that love Him.**"—BIBLE.

WHATEVER could inspire His breast
To place within that home of rest
Such beauties,—more than eye has known,
Or ever dreams of midnight shown.

It was His great delight, it seems,
To fill each space with love-lit beams,
That on the threshold, 'mid the throng,
Our joy would be one gladdened song.

Yet more and more, as on we trace
Those golden streets with steady pace,

Appears before the immortal eye.
Now could not look, 'cept we should die.

It pleased His Majesty on high,
To leave upfolded in the sky
The richest of His grandeur fair,
Until He chose to take us there.

Methinks we here enjoy surprise,
When once delights the ear, the eyes;
But from Omnipotent to spring,
What genius could an index bring?

We need not think that sweetest sounds,
And lovely greens, and flowery mounds,
And pearls, and shells, and diamond sand,
Are the prime mediums of that land.

They're far beyond the reach of thought,
Beyond the sphere of language taught,
Beyond the haze of earth, sea, air,—
No scenes on earth with them compare.

I've briefly run the prelude o'er,
And still would wish to speak of more;
But as such truths none could attain,
To 'tempt to tell them would be vain.

FINAL DESTINY.

"TIME gone, the righteous saved, the wicked damned,
And God's eternal government approved."—POLLOCK.

THE latest change is made at last,
The hurried scenes of time have passed;
The foaming crest, that misty main,
Can never dash its waves again.

The earth, the long 'ranged vernal seat,
At last did melt with fervent heat;
'T was on that great transaction day,
The earth, the heavens, fell away.

The final judgment had arrived,
When man—created man—revived;
The measure that he filled below
Was measured to him, as ye know.

The good, exulting in their King,
Responding with a new-fledged wing,
In heavenly airs divinely given,
When raised He them their souls to heaven.

The righteous, now forever free,
Unchanged, unchangeable to be,
Their lasting fame unmeasured, meet
The eye of God, assigned complete.

Around the throne, thrice happy there,
Do now the lofty millions share;
While numberless their glories roll,
And triumph fills the immortal soul.

There praise they God, and praise the Son,
The Holy Spirit, three in one;
Join and rejoin in matchless awe,
Devoted to His sovereign law.

The undeserving, 'neath His wrath,
Must bear the fury as He hath;
Beyond the place of goodness, they
Forever cast them all away.

Below the seat of hope and love,
Below those joyful scenes above,
Below, in night's beclouded doom,
They're fixed in everlasting gloom.

They broke the sovereign law of God,
Strayed from the path our Saviour trod;
Did not regard His holy day,
But sported, pleasured it away.

With swelling words, which fearless rose,
So base, so daringly, they chose
Home of the damned, this downward road;
At His command they there abode.

No Mediator to revive,
No Holy Spirit now to strive,
But, 'clipsed beneath His mystic spell,
Who holds the keys of death and hell,

Are there, wherein no sunbeams break,
No glittering stars their twinkling make,
No moon her pensive rays to throw,
To light the dark abode of woe.

So well deserve, for did not they
Throw every offered means away?
Reject, despise, blaspheme, control,
The powers that 'vade the undying soul?

Those powers that lead each one to share
An interest with their Maker there,
And gain for them that home of rest,
Where even God himself is blessed.

His love was boundless, free, complete,
Impressive, pure, in language sweet;
His gospel truths strove far and near,
That every list'ning ear might hear.

His Son, with arms extended wide,
Has purchased peace for all, He cried;
His blood was shed for each of you,—
What more could a Redeemer do?

Yet they would not abstain from sin;
They would not strive to enter in;
They would not love the God who gave
His Son a sacrifice, to save.

What further means could he extend
Than those he ever did commend?
His offered grace and mercy, sure,
Could all a privilege secure.

To die was not His wish they should,
Much rather all should come if would;
But selfish sins that govern host,
They ever seem to love the most.

What, then, if by His judgment they
Are now forever cast away,—
His righteous government did take
With sovereign justice to awake?

IMPARTIALITY:

MEANS OF ACCEPTANCE.

"Of a truth, I perceive that God is no respecter of persons. But in every nation, he that feareth Him and worketh righteousness is accepted with Him."—Bible.

Oh, mark ye well, benighted ones who dwell
on India's plain,
Or 'long the glistening waters deep, beside the
billowy main;
No matter where, or how thou art, or what
thy native clime,
Our Maker loves His own hand-work of every
name and time.
To you the truth, the sacred truth
Of pardoning grace is given;
And all who worketh righteousness
Will He accept in heaven.

Ye sovereign princes, common lords, of kingly
pomp and pride,
Luxurious in your homes of wealth, and in
your glory ride;
But not to your superior love was e'er trans-
ferred to be
A hallowed dawn, a holy day, an immortality.
But 'tis a truth, a blissful truth,
That pardoning grace is given;
And such as worketh righteousness
Will He accept in heaven.

All ye who roam on Afric's sands, or crowd
Pacific's coast,
Ye dwellers o'er the utmost sea, and all Japan
can boast,
For He, the builder of the world, is an impar-
tial God;
His matchless eye scans every place that ever
man has trod.
It is a truth, a gospel truth,
That sovereign grace is given;
And such as worketh righteousness
Will He accept in heaven.

Oh! spurn you not, ye fairest ones, the black man and the red,
Who share alike in summer sun, and by His hand are fed;
They of the gospel truth partake, and in the gospel share,
And others bless by blessings given to humble, fervent prayer.
For 'tis a truth, a sacred truth,
That pardoning grace is given;
And those who worketh righteousness
Will He accept in heaven.

The wise, the rich in wealth or fame, the unlearned, and the poor,
The halt, the maimed, the deaf or blind, are all alike secure.
If, from the heart the mind's engaged, and fearfully relies,
The weakest prayer is ne'er forgot nor lost in any wise.
Oh, for the truth, the hallowed truth,
That sovereign grace is given;
And such as worketh righteousness
Will He accept in heaven.

Why, then, in this enlightened land, this garden spot of earth,
Are there so many who neglect the work of countless worth?
The ideal fills the world below that lights the one above,
And myriad minions stamp the soul in characters of love.
Let not the false, deceitful foe
Absorb the grace that's given;
But work the works of righteousness
And dwell with Him in heaven.

Oh vain excuse! for vain 'twill be, when He from earth we call,
If we are unprepared to go to meet the Judge of all.
Far from the great arch'd throne on high, He sways o'er land and sea;
Salvation, too, to every soul He kindly offers free.
"Christ is the stone, the well-tried stone,
And a foundation sure;
And every soul that builds thereon
Will ever stand secure."

Now let us think, and thankful be for this so rich a day,
In which our happy lots are cast, and all commands obey.
Live holy, wisely, truly well, that we, like Abraham,
When called, as spotless may appear before the great "I AM."

Oh, bless'd the way, the living way,
The privileged way that's given,
That all, by works of righteousness,
May find a home in heaven.

INEFFICIENCY OF THE MOON AND SUN,

IN COMPARISON WITH THE GLOW OF HIS MAJESTIC GREATNESS.

"THEN the moon shall be confounded, and the sun ashamed, when the Lord of Hosts shall reign in Mount Zion, and in Jerusalem, and before His ancients gloriously."—BIBLE.

How shall appear, abashed, O Sun,
With all thy sparkling ray,
If then thou seem'st as even now,
When 'thwart the threshold lay.
Long hast thou reigned, thou glitt'ring orb,
And lit from pole to pole
This starry sphere from year to year,
Round as the planets roll.
Still, when the Lord of Light shall reign,

What were thy light, O Sun?
Thy radiant beams as clouded o'er,
Thy brilliancy outdone.
So shalt thou seem, as 't were, ashamed,
For then so much the less,
Though here exalted king of day,
Thou 'lt be as nothingness.

Thou beauteous Moon, that dwells so high
Above the earth and air,
And breaks the darksome shades of night
With thine own silvery glare,
Unconscious as thou seem'st to be,
What were thy worth, O Moon?
Ten thousand times ten thousand more,
Still numberless thy boon.
Yet what are thou, delightful Moon,
With all thy gentle glow,
And all thy light and loveliness,
That fills the world below?
For when appears the Lord of Hosts,
So matchless in His might,
Thou 'lt be as one confounded with
His store of golden light.

True Zion's king shall reign within;
Jerusalem shall see,
When once before His ancients, He
Shall reign most gloriously.
'T will be a one triumphant spell,
No chance nor change can break,
No angry wind, no cloud, can rise,
Or scene of sorrow wake;
For He, whose being is all light,
All glory to abound,
Will dwell among His chosen ones
With happiness profound.
He 'll let unveiled His glory then,
That every eye may see;
And every ransomed soul will share
The one eternity.

THE FASHION OF THIS WORLD.

"For the fashion of this world passeth away."—Bible.

Though the form of this world pass away,
And the garb that adorns us shall fade,
Yet methinks a still whisper speaks kindly:
"My love,
Thou shalt rest in a happier home above,
Where the clouds are changeless and the sun
is bright."
Farewell, earth, for that radiant light.

Though each orb has its mantle of ray,
So beautifully glowing and bright,
Yet methinks there's a world that's more lovely
and fit,
Where the loved ones, the ransomed, in ecstasy sit;

Where the air is fragrant and the sweet notes
chime.
Farewell, earth, for that radiant clime.

Though the musings of this life shall subside,
And the gems that adorn it shall fall,
Yet methinks we are bidden, are welcomed, my
love,
To those happier courts in heaven above,
Where the streamlets flow in their silver light.
Farewell, earth, for that radiant height.

Though the parting of earth we may greet,
And may welcome the last sounding bell,
Yet methinks there's a thought that will steal
o'er thy breast:
"How unworthy am I of that peaceful rest,
Where each breeze is freshened by the hand
that's fair."
Farewell, earth,—may I meet Him there.

THE PROMISED LAND.

WHEN shall we rest in the promised land?
When kept secure with the happy band?
Will it be when the spring breezes blow,
When the snow melts and the waters flow,
And swell their deep currents round the hills,
And leak away into little rills?
We know not, we know not when.

Will it be when the trees put forth bud and bloom,
When the warbling birds their notes resume?
When the grass is fresh on hill and vale,
And the lambs frisk in the whistling gale?
Then, shall we reach the happy shore,
Where parting scenes shall be no more?
We know not, we know not when.

Will it be when the long summer days arrive,
And the brilliant sun, with the showers, revive
The withered grass and drooping flower,
And send sweet cheers to each lovely bower?
Will it be when the reapers are gathering fast
Their plenteous harvest of wealth e'er cast?
  We know not, we know not when.

Or will it be when the summer is past,
And the leaves in autumn fall thick and fast;
When the whistling winds curl round and round,
And bring with each the echoing sound,
That winter is nigh, with its mellowing sigh,
That riper days have passed them by?
  We know not, we know not when.

Will it be when the snow has sheeted the earth,
And concealed from our view the mossy turf;
That brings to our ears the sounding bells,
The glad old tune that jingling tells?
Then, shall we see the happy shore
Where parting scenes shall be no more?
  We know not, we know not when.

It will be when the whispering voice from above
Gathers round us in stillness, pity, and love,
Enwreaths our fond spirits and bears them away
To those bright, sunny regions in glittering
array.
Then we shall rest in the promised land;
Then kept secure with the happy band;
It will be, it will be then.

THE PARABLE OF JOTHAM.

THE trees went forth in friendship kind,
As if with trunk and twig combined,
To nominate the Olive tree,
If but her highness would agree;
And thus her sacred trust avow,
Her well-sought guardianship allow;
And, "Like a king with godly prowess,"
Said they, "Wilt thou reign over us?"

THE OLIVE:

Should I my fatness leave, wherewith
By me they honor God and man,
To be a ruler over trees?
The answer is not that I can.

Then spake the trees again,—to whom?
To the fair Fig in noblest bloom,
As if to find in her some place,
Some hope, some glow of winning grace,
Whereby with skillful thrust could 'chieve,
And with one conquering word believe;
  Now like a king with godly prowess,
  Come thou, and rule thou over us.

THE FIG:

  Should I my sweetness here forsake,
  My fruit and all my good forego,
  To be a ruler over trees?
  Howbeit, still, I answer, No!

Then spake the trees unto the Vine,
With her grand tendrils to entwine;
Perchance they could invoke her pride,
On the fair wing of Time's swift tide,
And ultimately stand upright,
And rule the sturdy nation quite:
  Thus like a king with godly prowess,
  Come thou, and rule thou over us.

THE VINE:

Should I my wine now leave, by which
I cheer both God and man,
To be a ruler over trees?
The answer is not that I can.

Yet once again, said all the trees,
To the low Bramble, rich with leaves:
From thine own humble sphere extol
Thyself as monarch over all;
Do thou,—'tis with confiding trust
We fainly ask thee, for thou must,—
Do, as a king with godly prowess,
Come thou, and rule thou over us.

THE BRAMBLE:

If over you to reign I must,
Then in my shadow you must trust;
If you do not, let wild fires run,
And spoil the trees of Lebanon.

THE TWO TALENTS.

ONE talent small,
And is this all,
That's barely given me,
To sate the brain
In loss or gain,
Where should be two or three?

My cross I bear
Of toil and care,
A burden though it be;
One cheerless song,
The full hour long,
Is ever sung by me.

I stop to choose,
And then I lose
Myself in wild disguise,—

I fear the ill,
I feel the chill,
And thus my conscience lies!

My soul demands
My heart and hands,
Whatever be my lot,—
One talent small,
If this be all,
So I can bury not.

My feelings burn,
My soul I spurn,—
Such claim a talent one;
This pride of life,
With all its strife,
'T were better I had none.

Swift in a rage,
With soul engage
I would,—but turned to woo,
When to my right,
Just then in sight,
Was plainly pictured two.

A voiceless dove,
As from above,
Disclosed this peerless ray;
Myself I saw,
As without law,
Was grov'ling in the clay.

My talent two
I saw it new;
My soul give I to the;
And now I own
That thou alone
Art sovereign Lord of me!

RESPONSE TO AN INQUIRING BROTHER.

I THINK of that better land, dear boy,
I think of that better land;
With love's triumphant wing upborne,
And Faith's all-seeing eye,
I look away from transient scenes,
To those beyond the sky.
For there's a firmament of love;
Fix thy treasured home above.

I think of that pleasant home, dear boy,
I think of that pleasant home,
Where undivided comforts are,
Unhappiness unknown.
A home, ten thousand times more dear
Than any yet our own.

For there's a firmament of love;
Fix thy treasured home above.

I think of that peaceful rest, dear boy,
I think of that peaceful rest,
Where friendship dwells in every heart,
And lisped by every tongue,
In holy confidence to Him,
From whom all beings sprung.
Oh! for that firmament of love;
Fix thy treasured home above.

Think on thy parting day, dear boy,
Think on thy parting day;
For life with all its scenes shall close,
Its busy joys and care,
Then guide thy steps with watchfulness,
And find a welcome there.
High is that firmament of love;
Be there thy treasured home above.

THE WEEPING MOTHER.

WHY weep you, mother, o'er the departed dead?
Why linger round the sleeping bed?
Hath not the spirit that once mingled sweet
Fled from thy presence with anthems to greet
The highlands of heaven and angels, to bear
The record of thy daughter there?
Why, why weep you here?

Why send you longings for that much loved one?
Know you not that her work is done?
This lower world hath she not left, to share
Heaven's starry richness with the godly there?
Do there not myriads on the threshold stand,
To welcome to the promised land?
Why, why weep you here?

Why are you thus with deep sorrow oppressed?
Know you not she's gone to rest?
Hath she not parted with this trifling mirth,
And welcomed the return of Mother Earth?
And hath she not heard, too, with joyous taste,
Come, daughter, from the dreary waste?
Why, why weep you here?

Why should you be in sore anguish distressed?
Know you not she's with the blest?
There hath she not joined the angelic throng,
With swelling notes of an undying song?
And does she not long to embrace thee there,
And all the realms of heaven share?
Weep, weep ye no more.

THE SABBATH.

How fair and beauteous is the day,
When toils and cares are thrown away,
To sit and muse on things divine;
His works of goodness, oh! how kind.

To ponder o'er the gift of grace,
The glow that lights His smiling face,
And trust His love, and promise too;
His gift of mercy, oh! how true.

Fain would I count His wonders o'er,
And work and worship Him the more,
And of His truth and wisdom gain.
His loving kindness, oh! how plain

It's stamped on every bush and tree,
On every leaf that swings so free;

On every tiny blade of grass
His tender beams of love are cast.

The little flowers that bloom so gay
His unbought loveliness display;
And every pearly gem, so dear,
Portrays His kindness, oh! how clear.

The breeze, the atmospheric air,
That fans so freely everywhere,
If understood, does plainly tell
His loving kindness, oh! how well.

But tongue, the instrument of speech,
Is much too seldom known to speak
To praise in either word or song,
Still, in his kindness, oh! how strong.

WRITTEN ON THE DEATH OF MY MOTHER.

I CANNOT see dear mother now,
For mother she is dead.
Her words in solemn accents fell,
When, on her dying bed,
I heard her utter words of love,
With cold and feeble lip,—
Her sunken eye and marble brow
With sympathy were lit,

She scarcely seemed like mother then,
And yet I knew 't was her,
And oft in thinking of that hour
Does grief my memory stir.

When there I stood beside her couch,
A feeble minstrel, I,
So solemnly an impress told,
That mother dear would die.

How could it be? It seemed so hard
I knew no words to say.
I wondered why the living God
Should take her soul away.
Still well I knew the angel Death
Would come at His command;
He came, and took my mother dear
Up to Immanuel's land.

Her dying breaths were short and few;
I counted every one.
And soon I knew the trying fact,
That mother's work was done;
Her soul, unfettered and unbarred,
Was lost to human view;
There, where the weary cease from toil,
Has gone my mother, too.

Then, could I wish her back again?
    Oh! yes, I did, 't is true.
But now I only ask my God
    To know His will to do;
To feel that He who rules the world,
    From east to distant west,
Will throw His matchless arm around,
    And whisper, "All's for the best."

THE TEAR-DROP.

"In trouble and in grief, O God,
Thy smile hath cheered my way;
And joy hath budded from each thorn
That round my footsteps lay.

"The hours of pain have yielded good,
Which prosperous days refused;
As herbs, though scentless when entire,
Spread fragrance when they're bruised."

Liquid drops of crystal brightness,
Out the windows of the soul,
Now and then are seen to gather
Newly from the fountain's goal.

Were it harsh and cruel accents,
Lisped by some inhuman tongue?
Breathed the burden of some horror,
Wildly with confusion flung?

Be it thus, oh! foolish nature;
  Stoop to fiendish ills that sway;
Know you not where is another
  Faultless Harbinger of day,

Marks the wreck of weary pilgrims
  Wand'ring through a vale like this;
Gives to heart His Spirit holy,
  In this world of worldliness?

Ne'er distrust the hand of Greatness,—
  Goodness 'tends thee all the while,
Fresh from out the fount of Freedom,
  Where no kindred hearts beguile.

Every tie on earth be severed,
  Every seeming friend expel;
Still Jehovah reigns eternal,
  And He doeth all things well.

Mourn thou not, thou blighted spirit,
  Though thy state be sad and low;
Thou wilt, ere long, dawn immortal,
  Where life's cares can never go.

Ever languid, cheerless creature,
  Mock not at His high decree;
Worship at His shrine, adore Him,
  And His home thy home shall be.

Liquid drops of crystal brightness
  Shut out part the light of day;
Yet thy vision gleams with wonder,
  And thy heart hath words to say.

Oft appears the little tear-drop,
  Oozing from its tiny cell;
Careless in its downward flowing,
  But some hidden stories tell.

It may be of joy or sorrow,
  Each time differing in their sphere;
Yet there's that of moment, note ye,
  When is gushed the flowing tear.

'T is by means that we are moulded,
  Changed according to His will;
Sovereign speaks, but silent only,
  Though some means are sharp and shrill.

Check not, then, the little tear-drop,—
  Good, perhaps, that it were there;
Else thy seeing eye might wonder,
  And thy soul be waste and bare.

Better, far, thy mind's eye gather
  Little gems to deck thy brow
In the paradise of glory,
  Where no beauties fade as now,

Than be fed with joyous phantoms,
  Pleasing as the summer light,
Fading as the leaves of autumn
  Frosted by the wintry blight.

Aid me by thy spirit holy,
  Strengthen whilst on life's highway;
Ever guide me by thy counsel,
  Faultless Harbinger of day.

Then, when weary days are ended,
  All and every care gone by,
Every tear that shall have gathered
  Thou wilt wipe from sorrow's eye.

DEAR MARIA.

DEDICATED TO MISS MARIA BRONSON,—second daughter of Rev. Dr. BRONSON,—while on her way to Assam, India.

WE would not hold you back, dear girl,
Go where your duty lies;
Your hope is not for worldly gain,
But bliss beyond the skies.

Go! labor where the loved one wrought,
In Assam's far off land;
Cheered by her cherished memory,
Amid that stricken band.

Though many bitter ills assail,
Still may your prayers ascend,
And may you trust with constancy
Your Father and your friend.

An earthly father, too, you have,
  A counselor and guide,
Who soothes an orphan, called to be
  A helper by his side.

Your bark is now upon the sea,
  And tossed from wave to wave!
We ask protection from the Hand
  Whose power alone can save.

Beyond we see an humble cot,
  A home in heathen land,
Where many, many thousand now
  In Pagan darkness stand.

There go! there labor, teach and guide
  The wayward and the blind,
In paths of peace, to our Beloved,
  The friend of humankind.

Should years of weary toil be yours,
  Where care its shadow flings,
The Son of Righteousness shall rise
  With healing on His wings.

What peace the Gospel promise bears
An aching heart to stay,
When sorrows drear beset your path
In distant lands away!

Most blest will be your joyous lot,
When graves give up their dead;
Your brow bedecked with many stars,
For those to Jesus led.

Then gladly can you labor on,
Sure of immortal bliss
That shall repay all sorrow borne
In such a world as this.

A SENTIMENT.

IF the fondest hopes that thicken,
  Wedding future to the past,
And the golden chain that links them,
  Should with tears be overcast,
It betokens no remembrance
  Of some wild or rude display;
For in sunshine, as in sadness,
  There are tears to wipe away.

If the beam of love, once glowing,
  Should be abstruse, faint with grief,
And the gayer hours have vanished,
  As the dew upon the leaf,
It betokens no assurance
  That the boon has ceased to bloom,
For that richer gift may blossom
  'Neath a cold and silent gloom.

IF LOVE ALONE.

"ALAS for Love, if this be all,
And naught beyond, O Earth!"

IF love on every feature dwell,
In all that lisping tongue could tell,
Our every pearl or glittering gem
Seem as a royal diadem,
It would not reach within the veil,
But perish on a single gale.

If love for self and love for man
Were wrought in one protracted span,
With every tint of azure hue
That's hid in Time's remotest blue,
It would not bound on heavenly height,
But sink in everlasting night.

If love, that love-wrought kindle tie,
So prevalent beneath the sky,
Was wreathed in garlands rich and fair,
Perfumed on every breath of air,
It could not reach the sunny side,
In immortality to hide.

If love and friendship wove a name
That could secure a triple flame,
And to its shrine whole nations bow
In joyous triumph, even now,
Such fumes could never reach the Throne,
But perish in the world alone.

If love alone, or love confined
To this contracted space combined,
And gatherings from all seas and land,
Comprise a massive, loving band,
'T would then be sad, how sad the bliss,
If naught beyond a world like this.

I WOULD NOT BE WITH LOVE NOT FOUND.

"Though I speak with the tongues of men and angels and have not love, I am but sounding brass and tinkling cymbal.

"And though I have the gift of prophecy, and understand all mysteries and all knowledge, and though I have all faith so that I could remove mountains, and have not love, I am nothing."—Bible.

If I could speak with graceful tongue,
Had all the ills of nature flung,
Had all that mortals here can share
Of choicest treasures, rich and rare,
And to my eye so fitly changed,
Not one small title disarranged,
Still, without love, I should be found,
Like tinkling brass, an empty sound.

If I by wisdom could discern
The many lessons yet to learn,
And pen them down for great and small,
Heroic mistress of them all,
And from these draughts erect a name
Unequaled on the mount of fame,
Still, without love, I should be found
Like tinkling brass, an empty sound.

Could I by selfish words control
The very substance of the soul,
Or with gigantic skill possessed
The noblest eloquence and best,
And bore it with a princely tread
O'er common nature, quiet bred,
Still, without love, I should be found,
Like tinkling brass, an empty sound.

Were all my life clear as the sun,
My every act in candor done,
Should clothe the poor, the hungry feed,
And do all else to those in need
That would secure and animate
True knowledge, virtue most elate,

Still, without love, I should be found,
Like tinkling brass, an empty sound.

If I had faith, such faith to prove,
As could the great, huge mountains move,
Or scan all mysteries new and old,
As common millions ne'er unrolled,
And Hope, the friend of Faith, should stay
With double prop 'long life's highway,
Still, without love, I should be found,
Like tinkling brass, an empty sound.

ONE OF MY DAYS ALONE.

WELL, so it is a cloudy day;
  My heart is cloudy too;
And from my eyes the glist'ning tears
  Are falling fast to view.
I see, amid the gathering blight,
  The forms of those I love,
Transplanted from this prison world,
  To that bright world above.
O sacred Judge, O love divine,
Transfer me to that world of thine.

I feel the chilling blasts of earth
  Encircle round me here;
Cares, disappointments, rage without,
  And sorrows draw so near;

Yet I can hope as those have hoped,
  Those who have gone before;
For love still lingers on the breeze,
  And hopes on mercy's shore.
O sacred Judge, O love divine,
Transfer me to that world of thine.

No fragrant scent perfumes the air;
  The flowers have ceased to bloom,
But dream within the night-hours' watch,
  Of flowers beyond the tomb.
More pleasant 't is by far to know,
  'T is not as here to-day;
For there, within the spirit land,
  All tears are wiped away.
O sacred Judge, O love divine,
Transfer me to that world of thine.

There is a Hand sustains me here,
  And strengthens all my peace;
For He who bid'st the tempest roar
  Did bid the tempest cease.
Most happy we, to us these words
  Found in the Book of yore

Established to expel our gloom,
By his majestic lore.
O sacred Judge, O love divine,
Transfer me to that world of thine.

As snow-flakes, falling from the clouds,
And by the winds are driven,
So men, as by the breath of God,
Are carried up to heaven.
Delightful world? O King of kings,
Reserve within Thy bower,
All mine to soul-retiring rest,
When death decides the hour.
O sacred Judge, O love divine,
Transfer me to that world of thine.

Let deep within my mem'ry dwell
The debt of love I owe,
That when the breath of God is sent
I'll be prepared to go.
What kind memento can I leave,
What requiem can be given,
When I from out this prison world
Am carried up to heaven?
O sacred Judge, O love divine,
Transfer me to that world of thine.

THE SAINTED VISITANT.

WHILE in the shade of twilight dim,
  When the sun had gone to rest,
A whisper from a sainted one,
  From out the realms celest',
Was pierced into my silent ear,
  And in the secret soul,
The fullness which can't realize
  Until I reach the goal.

While in the shade of twilight dim,
  When the gentle whisper came,
A form seemed bending over me
  As she lisped each pensive strain,
I knew it was my mother dear,
  Who'd come again to earth,
With a pure and holy aspect bright,
  A clear and stainless worth.

In hand she held a golden staff,
  A life-crown on her brow,
And the splendor of her glowing face
  Is with me even now.
I list to catch each accent as
  It fell from love's own light;
For seraph whisperings they were,
  The whispering of delight.

'T was sweet to learn her exit to
  That better land afar
Was so elate with radiance,
  She left the gate ajar.
It was with seraph, sacred notes,
  And glitt'ring, golden plume,
They bore her angel spirit there,
  Up through the azure dome.

Their lays were so ecstatic that,
  With plumes which shone so bright,
She knew that they were bearing her
  To starry realms of light;

Amid ethereal pleasures fair
  That crown the saints above,
There soon she saw her Father's face,
  And dwelt with him in love.

Where glories of the heavenly world
  Do so caress the ear,
And love, life-giving orison,
  Heard never-ending year,
That sweetest, purest, loveliest lays
  Here 'neath the heaven's sung
Are but as transient wild-flowers found
  Beside the vernal sprung.

I asked, could I accompany her
  To that celestial sphere?
But with a mother's tender love
  She wiped away my tear,
And kindly urged me stay awhile,
  To fill my task of love;
'T were those, she said, who dwelt in court,
  And filled the aisle above.

Th' entreaties of that sainted one
From out the world of light
To me were quite sufficient with
The star of faith in sight;
For by its light, with steady tread,
Shall one day reach the goal
Where the glories of that better land
Will light the secret soul.

While in the shade of twilight dim,
In trembling awe I woke;
For th' angel, sainted visitant,
A tender farewell spoke.
Then through the fragrant-scented air,
And with a golden plume,
She slowly, calmly, took her flight
Up through the azure dome.

TO MY FRIEND, H——.

'T was here, along life's labyrinth,
  Each other's gaze we met,
And happy to my heart and mind,
  Each social feeling let;
It almost seemed a wonderment
  Another one I 'd find,
Thus fashioned nearly like myself,
  Or like my fav'rite kind;
I did not once suppose 't would be
  When strangers round me dwelt;
But oh! how cherished is the fact
  That disappointment's felt!

And thus along life's labyrinth
  We 've rambled for awhile,
And pleasantly the hours have passed,
  For love around did smile.

These love-lit scenes of joy and pride,
  Those hours of friendship sweet,
Those hasty moments, how they've flown,—
  Those moments, oh! how fleet;
As they have passed, may others still
  As dear, still dearer, be;
And when away, one thought I 'll urge,—
  That you'll remember me.

Here, traveling 'long life's labyrinth
  With mingled hopes and fears,
I 'll view the pleasures that have passed,
  And wipe away my tears.
And you, my dear and social friend,
  In lonely hours may weep,
But Hope, supporter of the soul,
  Will living embers keep.
You need not ask if in my heart
  You 'll still remembered be,
For were I ne'er to meet you more,
  You'd be in mind by me.

I 've parted thus with many a friend,
  Delightful, pure, and true;

Have sighed to have them far away,
  And so 't will be with you.
Be pleasures e'er your joyous lot,
  And happiness your doom;
A balm to soothe each touch and pain,
  Aud peace beyond the tomb.
How soon that tender farewell comes;
  Soon parted we must be;
But once again the thought I 'll urge,
  That you 'll remember me.

THE THIRD FLOWER.

WE'LL bless the day, if thus it be
  Again on life's fair flower
That beam of fond affection shines,
  To cheer this lonely hour.

We hope 't is well; may every glow
  Of bliss around you smile;
That everything on earth be sweet,
  And naught that sweetness guile.

Fair flower, he caught in early doom,
  To know a mother's care;
Fair flower, endowed with timely gifts,
  To spend in fragrance there.

A pleasant home, a friendly hand,
  A kind and willing heart,

Feed on the manna of His word,
  Till death alone can part.

Tend carefully that husband dear,
  To solace every pain;
His fleshly frame is frail indeed,
  He may not long remain.

Yet cannot know the will of Him
  Whose loving acts demand,
But humbly trust He 'll hold him in
  The hollow of His hand.

Preserve him still till other days,
  Till other years be done,
Before his heroic spirit's called
  Beyond the setting sun.

Be good unto that precious boy,
  Your husband's fondest care;
Teach him, in accents soft and meek,
  To heed a father's prayer.

Teach him to know a mother's pride,
  Teach him against whose breast
His infant head bent droopingly,
  His eyelids closed to rest.

Sweet babe, to know no more the smile
  That lit her starry eye,
But from that love-lit home was borne
  To mansions in the sky.

So strange, when bliss and pleasantness,
  Bestowed on all about,
The wave of death dashed to and fro,
  To eke her being out.

That lovely flower, that being fair,
  Surrendered to the doom,
But died to live and bloom again,
  Away beyond the tomb.

Mourn not, the ways of God are just;
  He hears with earnest care;

He, by His providence and love,
Has placed another there.

Then heed, fair flower, such place betook,
And every duty tend;
Tend kindly, truly to a word,
Till life itself shall end.

HAPPY NIGHT.

Oh! happy thought, that while we sleep,
The holy, sacred angels keep
Their silent watch about our bed,
With their pure white wings overspread.

Then sweet to sleep; no thought can break
The peaceful spell till morn shall wake;
But rest while in the shade of night,
Cared for and loved with true delight.

Oh! happy night, oh! social rest,
That makes our being seem most blest,
Most blest indeed, for midnight air,
Issues no sorrow or despair.

I say then, oh! how sweet to sleep,
A placid joy that seems so deep,

And truly one to tranquilize,
Until the new-born sun doth rise.

And thus it is, good reason we
Should ever, ever thankful be;
Praise Him, the all preserving One,
And feel to say "Thy will be done."

THE STILL SMALL VOICE.

In vain the whistling wind may pierce,
And force its current wild and fierce,
And rend the branches of the oak,
Terrific in their winding stroke;
'T will ne'er disturb my meek allay,
Nor waft my solitude away.
    Yet to me one sound is dear;
    'T is the still small voice I hear.

Though hard may beat the falling rain,
And dash against the window-pane,
And from the wood-trough eaves may pour,
The deluge as of cataracts' roar;
'T will never break my tranquil rest,
Nor rouse my tenement at best.
    Yet to me one sound is dear;
    'T is the still small voice I hear.

The splendor of the infant tongue,
When joyously their notes have sung;
More precious still the voice of glee
When prancing round the mother's knee.
In life's green spring, these notes would 'thrall,
Now own I miss them more than all.
        Yet of all on earth most dear,
        'T is the still small voice I hear.

WRITTEN ON THE DEATH OF A PHYSICIAN.

I CANNOT see how that dear friend can be dead,
Who watched o'er so carefully the sufferer's bed.
But we know he has gone, for the high One has
spoken;
We ne'er can recall him,—the bowl it is broken.

I know that our God, who in wisdom is just,
And He in whom all here can safely put trust,
Has spoken, has called him from life's busy throng,
To a heaven where purity rests not with wrong.

He has gone, he has tasted realities now,
The death-pallor's fixed on his beautiful brow;

He has passed through the valley, the shadow
that lies
Between this cold earth and that home in the skies.

We can think of him now in that heaven of rest,
Where the sad can look up and the weary are blest,
Where the radiant beams from the bright star are
shed,
And the numbers there gathered have silently fled.

It does seem so strange to think he is there,
Away with those millions, away from this care;
We feel we have missed him, will miss him still
more,
For his days now are ended, his labors are o'er.

I ask who'll not grieve for that friend who has fled,
Who watched o'er so tenderly the sufferer's bed;
But alas! he has gone, for the high One has
spoken;
We ne'er can recall him,—the bowl it is broken.

TO MY AUNT.

IN COMPLIANCE WITH HER REQUEST.

I KNOW of nothing better, Aunt,
  To speak to you in love,
Than tell you of that better land,
  That better land above.
You know full well the blooming rose
  That buds beneath the sun,
The many, many cares that screen
  Whilst we this journey run;
Screen from those rays of glory bright,—
  Those heavenly rays I mean,—
Those tinted hues of blissfulness,
  Where Christ and love are seen.

I need not wish to slide the veil
  That curtains it from me,

And catch a perfect glimpse of love,
  To tell it all to thee.
Tell of that purer land of light,
  That land of heavenly love,
The rivulets and the diadems,
  That cluster far above.
The happy home, the peaceful shore,
  The shore of quiet bliss,
The blissful rest for weary ones,
  Superior to this.

The little spark that glimmers near,
  Bears a delightful hue,
Bears pilgrims to their lasting home,
  Their everlasting view.
It will suffice, it need not be
  More brilliant here below,
To lead you through the trackless wilds,
  And purer mercies show.
Shows how the all-alluring One
  Invites the gentle gale,—
Invites you to that better land,
  The land within the veil.

I'm sure you'd love that land, Aunt.
 There lovers never fail;
There passports are already sealed
 Within the happy veil.
There unknown pleasures never cease,
 There joys transparent flow,
Flow in one living, boundless stream,
 There ever, ever glow.
Prepare thy heart, take rest awhile,
 He'll loudly call for thee;
When in the startling, echoing sound,
 Let *peace* thy calling be.

These lines are written by a friend,—
 A social friend indeed,—
A friend whose every act may prove
 To be a friend in need.
I love to write with feelings calm,
 With feelings kind and pure;
It binds within the feeble frame,
 Such as may long endure,
Binds love, unwreathed with giddy mirth,
 Substantial and sincere;
And makes the form seem eloquent,
 As we commingle here.

THE DEAF GIRL'S LAMENT.

A BEAUTIFUL and lovely tree
 Beside the window grew;
I see its leafy branches swing,
 As something tall and new,
But know there is a something more,
 I have not quite forgot:
There is a sound among the leaves,
 But oh! I hear it not.

The little birds upon the wing,
 I see them 'light around;
Can only watch them as they fly,
 Or perch upon the ground.
But know there is a something more,
 I have not quite forgot:
They sweetly sing their little song,
 But oh! I hear it not.

The groves still have their pleasant shades,
  And I'd delight to be
One of the thousand ones who roam
  In sweet tranquility.
But know there is that something more
  I have not quite forgot:
The whistling of a joyous song,—
  But oh! could hear it not.

I see the dearest friends unite,
  And eye bespeaks to eye;
And by the move of ruby lips,
  They all to each reply.
But know there is a something more,
  I have not quite forgot:
A voice like music fills the room,
  But oh! I hear it not.

I see the little ones at play,
  And think they're happy too;
I watch them in their childish sport,
  With beating heart and true.
But still there is that something more,
  I have not quite forgot:

The ringing of their merry laugh,—
  But oh! I hear it not.

There is a good, a beautiful,
  For every heart a home;
Life borders on elysium, though
  I'm wearied and alone.
I know too well there's something here,
  It is not all forgot:
A something of elysian fair,
  But oh! I heed it not.

WRITTEN ON THE DEATH OF AN INFANT.

THOU art gone, thou art gone, gentle babe,
  Whom so fondly thy mother embraced,
Away from those smiles so oft mingled with tears,
  Where all seasons of sorrow's erased.

Thou art gone, thou art gone, gentle babe,
  To that land where the sun ne'er shall set;
Where the dayspring has cast her full lustre of
    light,
  And its beauty thou will'st ne'er forget.

Thou art gone, thou art gone, gentle babe!
  Kind angels are tending thee now;
There hallow'd thy rest on His bosom most bless'd,
  And thine like the seraphim's brow.

Thou art gone, thou art gone, gentle babe!
  Can bid but a silent farewell;
But the promise of God to His chosen is, that
  Of His, none shall ever expel.

Thou art gone, thou art gone, gentle babe!
  But know, sure, I shall meet you again;
For the love that is buried lies anchored in trust,
  A jewel of love to regain.

Thou art gone, thou art gone, gentle babe!
  Oh! how shall I ever express?
For the fountain that's stirred with the weakness
      of words
Few feelings of thought can egress.

Oh! sad heart, oh! sad heart, why repine?
  I would that thou could'st realize
And feel this affliction, this chastening, is but
  A blessing of love in disguise.

WHERE SHALL I FIND PEACE?

In the home I loved so well,
In the cottage in the dell,
'Long the streamlets pure and bright,
Cheerful as the summer's light?
There, is it there, Mother?

Is it in our country fair,—
Could we meet it anywhere?
'Long the wayside is it hedged?
Could it be 'mid tall grass pledged?
There, is it there, Mother?

Is it in our village bound,
Where the people seem all crowned,
Wreathed in splendor as they go,
Making such a gaudy show?
There, is it there, Mother?

Is it in some distant land?
Is it found on Afric's sand?
On some island in the sea,
Lovely, beauteous, and free?
There, is it there, Mother?

Is it in some region cold?
Is it where there's sands of gold?
Anywhere among mankind
Such a thing as peace to find?
Where, anywhere, Mother?

THE MOTHER'S REPLY.

It is not in the cottage,
Nor in the mansion fair;
No, not along the wayside,
Nor hedges anywhere.

It is not in our cities,
Not in our country found

It is not in our valleys,
  Nor anywhere around.

It is not on the islands,
  Nor far on Afric's sand;
Not in this sunny climate,
  Nor in a distant land.

'T is far beyond these dwellings,
  Beyond this earthly shore,
In that upper home of glory,
  Where midnight is no more.

'T is there, my darling daughter,
  Along those streamlets bright,
The boon of peace is perfect
  As the sparkling orbs of night.

There, fixed on yonder highland,
  A pledge of sacred trust,
A pledge of peace, my darling,
  From the Holy One and Just.

SEED-TIME.

Ye children fair and lovely,
  Whose hours go lightly by,
With th' glowing beams of morning
  Your path to over-sky;
Bear ye in sweet remembrance,
  While far from care and strife,
With the heart yet young and tender,
  'T is the seed-time of your life.

Ye gay and joyous-hearted
  With sunshine on your brow,
And the dew of youth distilling
  In crystal clearness now.
You should ever well remember,
  While free from care and strife,
While the heart is young and tender,
  'T is the seed-time of your life.

When the bloom of youth is opening
  Most exquisitely fair,
And the starry eyes are strangers
  To the world's bewitching snare,
Oh! bear in sweet remembrance,
  While unworn with care and strife,
The heart is young and tender,
  'T is the seed-time of your life.

And when the reaper's whetting
  His sickle quick and fast,
The wheat within to gather,
  And the tares without to cast,
May your golden sheaves be many,
  Tho' grown 'mid toil and strife,
From the planting deeply rooted
  In the spring-time of your life.

THE DYING GIRL.

"'T IS sweet, oh! sweet to die
When Jesus Christ is nigh,
For then the soul fears not to try
Her unfurled wings.
With firm and fearless flight
She soars into the night,
Knowing she soon shall reach the light
Heaven's morning brings."

"I AM going, I am going, I shall not be long,
And this tongue soon will lisp its latest song,
And this beating pulse will then cease to be.
Oh! shed not a tear, not one tear-drop for me.
"I'm going to the highland,
To the highland green and fair,
Where loved friends have met together,
And will know no parting there.

"I am failing, I am failing, I shall soon have fled
The death-damp is on me," the dying girl said,
As she raised her eyes with a calm look of love
As befitted for heaven as the angels above.
"And then upon the highland,
The highland green and fair,
We shall meet in love together,
And will know no parting there.

"I am sinking, I am sinking, but no sorrow is in sight;
All is love, pure and plenty, in the world of golden light;
And whilst upon the border, with faith's all-seeing eye,
I behold the promised beauties prepared beyond the sky.
"And there upon the highland,
The highland green and fair,
We shall meet in love together,
And will know no parting there.

I am going, I am going," and the word, "Farewell,"
Was the very last from her cold lips that fell;
And the poor dying girl sank away to rest,
As the orient sun that sinks in the west.
And then upon the highland,
The highland green and fair,
She had met in love together,
And will know no sorrow there.

She has gone, she has gone, and her form was laid
In the church-yard there, 'neath the old oak shade,
And over her grave may the green myrtle grow,
And the night winds murmur both soft and low.
But there upon the highland,
The highland green and fair,
She now dwells in love together,
And will know no parting there.

MY VALUED FRIEND.

My friend, I'm thinking of you now,
  And wonder where are you;
In life,—upon some well known spot
  To live,—and how you do.

Long months have passed, and even years
  Have too, since we last met;
But in the circling round of thought,
  You come to me as yet.

I see your slender form, your dark
  Blue eyes as times before,
And best of all, that kindly look
  Of love, I longed for more.

Do you remember well, one morn,
  When down the lane I came,
That burst of joy, so true?—well, now
  My heart is just the same.

That was a happy time,—I deemed
  It rich, and, too, I knew
Your heart was linked with mine the while,
  In all 't was just and true.

But for a cause best unexpressed,
  On earth was doomed to part,
Still deigned to each that love-wrought claim,
  That fastens heart to heart.

I'm glad for this, 't is good, 't is well,
  But would we could unite,
As used to do in by-gone days
  When all was free and right.

Cannot! It is a solemn thought,
  To think so it must be;
To only, o'er the long-linked chain
  Of miles, speak words for thee.

And too, I see, upon that once
  Fair brow are marks of care,
Drawn by the hand of time, such as
  Are here and everywhere.

Fain would I lend a gentle hand
  And give one soothing touch;
One sympathetic smile to cheer
  Your lone heart, or some such.

But th' dividing space affords, save
  An imaginary view,
Coupled with reminiscences
  Of the past, pure and true.

I've tho't and yearned for you, my friend,
  'Till the last gleam of day;
Now leave you to the remembrance,
  Of Him who loves alway.

THE VOICE OF GOD.

LINES written during a sweeping sickness, and many deaths, in the village of P——, March, 1864.

O! THINK ye of so strangely
  The sadness of our place,
As if unkind hands were bidden
  To lay our village waste?
To spoil the heads of fam'lies,
  To take the child away,
O, no, 'tis but the voice of God,—
  Of God who speaks to-day.

Oh! erring ones, why wonder,
  For He who places here,
Will null, or He 'll enliven,
  In ev'ry clime and sphere;

Must know that he requires,
  Inquired of will be,
The Omnipotent Jehovah,
  Our great Creator, He.

And know ye not He's willing,
  If waiting people pray,
To bless with long endurance,
  And spare them day by day?
  And well He knows if any
In wayward paths have trod,
  Can speak, for He's Jehovah,
Our great Creator, God.

'T is so, perhaps, that many,—
  And that is why He'd speak,—
Know not an under Shepherd,
  Nor the Royal Shepherd seek.
So by His sovereign power,
  Is heard the funeral knell;
Omnipotent hath spoken!
  He doeth all things well.

Awake, all ye inhabitants,
  Ye living here to-day,

And by these acts of Providence
  Be taught to watch and pray;
To know that a Redeemer
  Will ev'ry conflict see,
And though some scenes be darkened,
  He'll still remember thee.

SECOND MARRIAGE.

Written in view of my much esteemed friend, O. H. F——d, June 28th, 1863.

Your starry pilgrimage below
  Is fixed on earth again;
Such sacred scenes of social bliss
  In lovely altars lain.

I'm sure 't is most a happy lot,
  Where heart compares with heart,
And, hand in hand, together stand,
  In life no more to part.

'T is goodness God in mercy lends
  From yon celestial skies,
To knit faith, hope, and love, to be
  In such terrestrial ties.

With armor on, and "sun so clear,
  And He our lasting light,"
Whose sovereign mercy gave you aid,
  And strengthened your delight.

If blighted once by death's cold hand,
  And chilled your love's embrace,
'T was but your heavenly Father's will,
  To fill a holier place.

Can think of her in sunny climes
  Beyond a cloudless tomb,
In triumph, for her Saviour gave
  In Paradise a room.

Her latest breaths were notes of praise,
  And angels caught the sound.
Transparent, too, "her name she saw
  On Life's fair Book was found."

'T was thus she bade the world farewell,
  To join no more in word
With you in consecrated lays
  To our most glorious Lord.

Then for awhile you stood alone,—
  Alone 'mid scenes of time,—
Rejoicing in the light He gave,
  Reflected most sublime.

Pure words of truth you promptly told:
  You said to man, be wise,
Forsake, receive, rejoice, and go
  To mansions in the skies.

But blessed be a Father's will,—
  A will, too, like your own,—
That He another hand would give,
  Another heart would loan.

Now, bear her to your bosom close,
  Still leaning on His rod;
Support her o'er the hills of life,
  And lead her on to God.

To live, be praise your latest breath;
  Let angels catch the sound;
Transparent, too, your names enrolled
  On Life's fair Book be found.

MY NATIVE STATE.

THE morning sun I see arise
Resplendent in the eastern skies;
And in its light, as fine and fair
The flow'rets bloom, as anywhere.
The trees put forth their clustering leaves,
The harvests yield as goodly sheaves;
The running vines their 'bundance bear
Of fruit as choice, as rich and rare;
But though the fruit, the flowers, and sheaves,
The morning light and clust'ring leaves,
With all I try to love of late,
Still, best I love my Native State.

Here, too, each little liquid brook
Runs pure and clear at every nook,
And, by the rippling waters' flow,
The prickly shrub and wild flowers grow,

And music breaks the silent spell
O'er many a hill and fertile dell,
Borne fresh upon the fragrant air,
The same sweet melody as there;
But though the fragrant scented air,
And brooks as pure as anywhere,
And all I've tried to love of late,
Much best I love my Native State.

I find the poor with little store,
Still toiling on for little more,
And by the very same free light
The joyous with their means and might,
Make discount on the hourly space,
Where should be more assuming grace.
So, verily, the thing be true,
That some rich ones are poor rich, too.
But thou the ones with means abound,
The poor found everywhere around,
And all I try to love of late,
Still, best I love my Native State.

Most certainly there are some such
I love and care for very much;

Whose pleasant smiles and pleasing air
Would quell the dark hour of despair.
I feel to think and judge them true,
And prove it by the acts they do.
So, as the vine to twigs entwine,
Their loving hearts are linked with mine.
But though this love, these acts, this air,
And smiles to cheer me everywhere,
With all I try to love of late,
Much best I love my Native State.

Home of my childhood and my youth,
Where I was led in paths of truth,
Where duty bade my heart comply,
And pass the earth-born follies by;
Deep, deeper still my soul awakes,
And to the shad'wy vale it breaks,
Where lies a precious treasure hid
Down underneath the surface lid.
So dear to me that distant spot,
I'm sure 't will never be forgot;
And oft it seems my heart would break,
Still yearning for my Native State.

LITTLE TUDIE.

LITTLE TUDIE, how we love her!
  Precious little one is she;
Beauty on her brow is beaming
  With a glow of ecstasy.
Happiness is brooding round her,
  Round the little tottering one;
Hearts ne'er spoken half their pleasure,
  Seeming only just begun.
Yes, we love her. See her going,—
  Up and down her little feet;
Prattling, cooing, stumbling, falling,
  Over all she haps to meet.
Then the mother, careful, tends her,
  Calls her "precious little chick,"
Wipes away the tear that's gathered,—
  Wonders if her babe is sick.

Hushed and soothed, all anguish over,
  Once again renews her pace,
Playfulness so plainly pictured
  In her little roguish face.
Always welcome,—father takes her,
  Gives a kindly, willing kiss;
With a heart of rapture glowing,
  Thinks he knows a world of bliss.
What a treasure in the household,—
  What aspiring joys impart,—
What a soft, momentous feeling,
  Binding past from heart to heart.
Sure there is no sort of pleasure
  Half as exquisite as this,
Half as lovely in its beauty,—
  Lovely as our Tudie is.
"I ask no more in joy or pride,
Than ever be my baby's guide."

A DREAM.

I DREAMED one night of a starry west,
And close to my view the vision press'd;
The stars that seemed at first but few,
As I longer gazed, in their number grew.

And soon arose such a halo there,
A beautiful bow, so bright and fair,
Some stars within, and some without,
That I looked with wonder the world about.

And the stars had a swiftly brightening glow
Till it seemed a flood over all below;
For their rays spread far, like the rays of the sun,
And I conned their glories one by one.

Then assurance came that those orbs were mine;
It gladdened my heart like a thing divine;

And my soul was full, and my pulse beat high,
As I stood alone 'neath a cloudless sky.

The bow was that of a golden hue,—
It had neither crimson, purple, nor blue;
So unlike the beauteous one in the cloud,
I watched and wondered, nor spake aloud.

The sight was a joyous one to see,
And I yearned to know if its sign might be
Of some long-waited better day
To dawn on me with its golden ray.

And then from my beautiful dream I woke;
Too soon I saw that the spell had broke;
We had nothing left, my soul and I,
Of the vision that sped like a meteor by.

But even now as I sit and write,
And think of the beautiful dream that night,
My soul with the happy hope is blessed
That my sun will set in a golden west.

THE HEART OF THE YOUNG.

If there is found a genial tie
  That bindeth heart to heart,
A link that's parallel with truth,
  To only love impart,
That hath a bearing, great or small,
  A bearing high or low,
Unshaken by the blasts of time,
  A concentrated glow,
A fascinating charm on earth,
  A filial beauty sprung,
'T is truly an unerring fact,
  Such are found in the heart of the young.

If there is joy and happiness
  Embosomed most complete,
And with a clear and tranquil gaze
  Each timely aspect greet;

Aspiring zeal sublimely hung,
  And hope to that extend,
With marked enthusiasm bold
  That makes the world amend,
Without a transient, wayward guile
  Amid the treasure flung,
It must be an unerring fact,
  Such are found in the heart of the young.

If true that there's a golden thread
  Entwines the human soul,
A three-fold cord that cannot break,
  Or cannot e'er unroll,
And hath, much like the jessamine,
  Full many a tangled clew,
And bearing fair and beauteous buds
  Enriched with early dew,
And whereupon is ever found
  A peaceful conscience strung,
It must be an unerring fact,
  That's found in the heart of the young.

If ever there is sense to feel
  Between the right and wrong,

A care to own the honest part,
  And lisp a joyous song;
To have a friend who will not fail,
  Though all beside should spurn,
And with effectual confidence,
  Each from the other learn;
When such like blissful influence rise,
  More glorious than the sun,
It must be an unerring fact,
  These are found in the heart of the young.

If happy thoughts are known to rise,
  Delightful all the day,
With never-ceasing joys to glide
  From morn till evening ray;
And if the lighted spirit seems
  Untiring as the moon;
The daisies sweet are all their own,
  A fragrant pathway boon;
And if with love-wrought melody
  Each cordial anthem rung,
'T is truly an unerring fact,
  These are found in the heart of the young.

THE OCEAN.

"ROLL on, thou deep and dark blue ocean, roll."
—BYRON.

THE dark blue ocean's ceaseless roar
Was just the same in days of yore.
Have critics e'er observed its sense,
And boasted of its eloquence?

That loud, deep roar, how passing sweet,
There where the bounding billows meet,
Whose foaming surf turns o'er and o'er,
And dashes 'gainst the rocky shore.

The dark blue ocean's just the same;
Though many have crossed its wat'ry main,
There is no track to mark their way,
For still the bounding billows play.

How harsh, how rude their gestures are!
How wide, how circling, and how far
From shore to shore their billows roll,
And spread their dance from pole to pole.

Lord Byron, on his lofty height,
Once stooped to quench his appetite,
Stooped to address the ocean's haze,
And loudly uttered forth its praise.

Dash on, thou dark and heavy mass!
Deep swelling current, onward pass;
Still dash, and roll from shore to shore,
And throw thy bounding billows o'er.

THE LONELY SISTER.

THE day has seemed long, and how can I stay,
Or sit alone longer, and have you away?
And will you not come, my sweet sisters, to me?
I am constantly wishing, am waiting for thee.

To the garden so green have I oft looked away,
And list to the singing birds, merry and gay;
But no flowers so fair, nor a song was so sweet
As to spoil me from longing my sisters to meet.

My feelings are sad, but I cannot refrain,
The tears that are flowing are flowing in vain,
For I know very well I am not yet to see;
Each prospect is blasted, is darkened to me.

Oh! why do you tarry and leave me to roam,
Or sorrow and pine mid the pleasures of home?

As if you could ne'er more enjoy a review
Of the scenes of your childhood, where love sparkled true.

The rain-drops are falling, have laden the grass;
I hear them now tapping so hard 'gainst the glass,
It seems they were tapping, were talking to me,
I would I could hear but a tapping from thee.

My spirit would triumph o'er sorrow that's past,
And leave it to linger and pine in the blast,
Whilst the beauties of gladfulness burst over me;
I then would be happy, sweet sisters, with thee.

But alas! I am here, like some poor, lonely guest,
And the sun it has sunk in the far distant west;
I have watched the dark shade as the night has drawn near:
Oh! come, my sweet sisters, I would welcome you here.

THE YOUNG BRIDE.

"My hope, my heaven, my trust must be,
My gentle guide, in following thee."

Here, on thy arm, sweet love, I lean,
And, like a garland fair,
Is woven my own dear soul to thee,
In the light of summer air.

Yes, I can fashion those glossy locks;
And ever by thy smile
May know the fullness of thy vast soul
Will never me beguile.

I'm sure I can trust in thee, my love,
And make thy heart my throne;
For, since by the light of thy pure eye,
My every care has flown,

I can follow thee o'er the sea of life,
  Whatever the tide may be;
And if the billowy waves run high,
  I am ever still with thee.

I know I can shelter beside thee, love,
  Where'er on earth thou art,
And feel forever more 't will be
  The dear home of my heart.

For, ever since my eye beheld,
  I chose thee for my guide;
And now on thy arm, sweet love, I lean,
  Thy own meek, cherished bride.

What further hope or heaven need be?
  Since, like a garland fair,
Is woven my own dear soul to thee,
  In the light of summer air.

THE BEGGAR BOY.

He came, alas! poor beggar boy,
  As poor as poor could be;
His wretched, dirty, tattered clothes
  Were wonderful to see.

As he upon the threshold stood,
  So tremblingly with grief,
One ray of hope was in his breast,
  And beamed for his relief.

I saw a bright, clear, crystal tear
  Course down his rosy cheek,
And, underneath those drooping lids,
  Eyes dove-like, soft and meek.

Those jetty locks, in wavy flow,
  A noble brow concealed;

And from his lips fell many a word,
  And many a truth revealed.

I need not tell all that he told
  Of misery and woe;
And, furthermore, I need not add
  The cause that made him so.

But from the lesson that he gave,
  And from his lonely air,
There fastened in my heart for him
  Deep, sympathetic care.

He sheltered with us in a cot
  Upon a lovely green,
And livelier grew the beggar boy,—
  More cheerful soon was seen.

'T was learned, ere years had rolled their round,
  Or even months had passed,
The virtue of the beggar boy
  Was most immensely vast.

He had it treasured in his heart,
  The fact he could not lie;
Or if a sinful act he did,
  His Maker, God, would spy.

So, in this true and holy way,
  He onward, upward grew,
Till scarce a man 'mong thousand men
  Seemed ever half as true.

His dwelling now is on a plain,
  A gothic, great and high;
God blessed the honest beggar boy
Who could not tell a lie.

And now, my little readers, you
  A goodly lesson learn:
Do as the little beggar boy,
  And every evil spurn.

IDEAS

THAT OCCURRED AFTER LEARNING OF MY FRIEND M——'S MARRIAGE VOW.

I SEEM to feel a something,
  A something in my heart,
And to my ears a whispering,
  That you and I must part.
I ask, Can this be surely,
  A tale like this so sad?
And can it ne'er allure me,
  And turn all sadness glad?
For thee I hope, most truly,
  A pleasant path through life;
Be to thy husband, wisely,
  A meek and loving wife.
I seem to think of bygones,
  Whilst thinking thus of thee;

Can all our cares be bygones,
  Each from the other free?
Could ever pinions flutter,
  And bear our love away?
A something seems to mutter,
  They never, never may.
Perhaps our days of pleasure
  Are very nearly o'er;
But in the eternal morrow
  There's parting never more.

Then must I form to mem'ry
  The by-gone days of yore,
And rest on nurtured energy
  I had so long before.
Come to me in the night-time,
  When cares are tossed away;
Yes, in the hush of midnight
  A silent visit pay.
Then when the sun has risen
  So beautiful and bright,
My mind will seem all freshened
  With solace of the night.

How often in our spring-time
  Would part to meet again;
But soon another meeting,
  The parting one of pain.
Though many walk beside me,
  The sparkling and the gay,
'T will seem all strange without thee
  To cheer my lonely way.
'T will seem as if my moments
  Of pleasure all were o'er;
But in the eternal morrow
  We 'll meet to part no more.

There is so much in lifetime
  Controlling to the mind,
So much we need remember,
  So much that seems to bind,
That, by and by, when changes,
  And new things have appeared,
And years roll on like ages,
  With many forms upreared,
Then would YOU quite forget me,
  And think no more of her

Who used so oft to greet you,
  And in your path occur?
But hush! I'll let another,
  Another voice than mine,
With deeper love than brother's,
  Close to your heart entwine.
How sacred be that tendril,
  Uniting two in one!
As precious as an em'rald,
  Enlivening as the sun,
From me you 'll part, thro' friendship,
  With beams of love still dear,
Like the far-off stars of heaven,
  May shine as bright and clear.

THE LITTLE ONES.

HAPPY children, all at play,
Cheerful as the summer day,
Round and round the parlor floor,
Playing "peep" at every door;
Rosy hue upon the cheek;
Bright eyes, looking soft and meek;
Health and beauty on each brow;
Joyous in their pleasures now.
    Well it interests my heart!
    Not that I would play their part,—
    Only that I wish, I say,
    I was innocent as they.

See them go the circle 'round,
With a merry shout and bound;
Silken tresses rise and fall,
Cov'ring forehead,—nearly all;

Underneath, a sunny smile,
Fair and beauteous the while,
Gladly spend the hours at play,
Little ones, in childhood's day.
    And it interests my heart!
    Not that I would play their part,—
    Only that I wish, I say,
    I was innocent as they.

Scores of happy visions spread,
To their hearts and minds are wed;
Soaring in their airy flight
Far beyond the reach of sight.
Yet, ah! yet they careless tread,
Heeding not the moments fled;
Onward in their sportive glee,
Gaily, weariless, and free,
    How it interests my heart!
    Not that I would play their part,—
    Only that I wish, I say,
    I was innocent as they.

FATHER'S OLD TUNE.

'MONG much and many things in store
That happened in the days of yore,
There's none more firmly fixed in mind,
Nor dearer would I wish to find,
Than that old tune so often hummed
When every hard day's work was summed.
  It went,—Chink chank, chink chank chinky,
      Chank chink, chink chank chink,
      Chank chinky, chank chink.

And as I leaf o'er memory's will
And read anew its pages, still
I find it so recorded there,
So plainly does my memory bear,
That I can truly hear and see
As when he took me on his knee:
  It went,—Chink, chank.

See how us children, clambering, clung;
Arms snug around his neck, we hung.
And when, at times, our foothold missed,
He soon replaced and kindly kissed.
Now this was as in days of yore,
And that old tune I have in store:
  It went,—Chink, chank.

Full many a long cold, wintry eve,
With tired aches, I now believe,
My dear and much-loved mother's stand
Was fraught with skilled work by her hand;
But father's hard day's work was summed,
So o'er again his tune he hummed:
  It went,—Chink, chank.

But now my mother's toils are done,
And all 't was love beneath the sun;
And father, with his furrowed brow,
Has different cares and sorrows now;
And though his hard days' works are summed,
We hear no more the tune he hummed,
  That went,—Chink, chank.

I NEVER LOVED BUT ONE.

I NEVER loved but one.
He came to me when first the blushing rose of girlhood
Had settled on my brow;
'T was when those giddy fancies curl
That break in sorrow now!
Break to be forever broken!
There is no change for me.
The gallant ones have spoken,
Have cast my lot from thee.

I never loved but one.
In humble tones of eloquence he breathed forth solemn vows
Drained from the heart's deep well;
The joy, the grief, that it has brought,
Eternity can tell.

Tell—can tell of hearts that are broken,
  Of hearts that are beating free;
Tell of one tender token,
  A token true from thee.

I never loved but one.
Let echoes lend a louder shrill, and teach in
  magic sound
Thy sweet, unerring voice;
'T is true thou art, though far away,
My early only choice.
  Choice—can choose no other, never!
    There is no change for me;
  The gallant ones did sever,
    Did cast my lot from thee.

MY THANKS.

THE guide who o'er so many miles
And cragged hills, and rugged piles,
Has safely kept me through these wilds,
I thank.

The bowed and feeble gray-haired man
Of tottering step and 'wildering plan,
Who cheers and aids as best he can,
I thank.

Her, who has felt life's keenest thorn,
Has long a crown of sorrow worn,
Yet soothes a spirit wrecked by scorn,
I thank.

Her, who in costly robes can shine
But still a list'ning ear incline,
And yielded sympathy divine,
I thank.

Her, who with youth's bewitching wile
Has buoyed my sinking heart the while,
And blessed me with a cheerful smile,
I thank.

Those who have proved to love me best,
Who chose me for their favorite guest,
And 'gainst my cheek their soft lips pressed,
I thank.

Those who have chased the cloud away,
Who bade my weary footsteps stay
Apart from sultry Summer's ray,
I thank.

Such as have done, or here or there,
A parent's part in love and care,
And breathed for me one fervent prayer,
I thank.

NIAGARA FALLS.

So HURRIEDLY, hastily, onward you go,
You heed not the howlings of wild winds or snow;
No rest on thy bosom, no bark on thy sea,
And one thy continuance thro' all ages shall be.

Thou wert form'd by Jehovah's most powerful hand;
He marked out the valley and piled up the land;
He filled in the water, a notable fact,
And established the flow of the great cataract.

Thou wert there ere a tree or a shrub ever grew,
Ere the hawk, or the owl, or the turtle-dove flew;
When the base of creation's foundation was laid,
Thy hard, rock-bound coast was effectually staid.

Thence onward thy course, with a measureless flow,
The foam keeping pace with the rapids below;
And the spray from thy breast, like the dew on
the hill,
O'er the moss-covered rocks has been ever distilled.

The eye of the red man once gazed with delight
As he stalked through the wood to thy borders
so bright,
From the hut or the wigwam, so proudly and bold,
To spy out thy sportings which ages have told.

Long years bring their changes at home and abroad;
The wild lands are tilled where the red man once
trod,
The haunt, with the hut, and the fierce beasts of
prey,
Alike, with the red man, have all passed away.

Yet bold is thy current, and onward to bear;
No spell has assuaged through the long ages there;
No change has arrested the wave curling free,
And one thy continuance thro' all ages shall be.

MY OLD BOX.

My dear old box, my treasure box, where things
both new and old
Are laid therein more carefully than glittering
pearls and gold;
And better far, to me, than they, for heart and
soul are there,
And, like the buoyancy of youth, it haunts me
everywhere.

It is the same, the very same,—I had it long ago,
And there, between those dingy sides, each little
scrip I stow;
When, now and then, it seems to give,—I almost
think it wrong,—
Pshaw! I take my needle bold and stitch the
corners strong.

There is no wreath, no golden leaves, nor flowery
sculptured mold,—
In fact, there's naught about the box that's worth
one grain of gold;
Old, homely, dirty, crooked, and scratched,—to say
I love it well,
Seems like some wild, romantic tale, that modern
sages tell.

The thought of how it looks, and is, is just as
good to me
As anything that man could make, or even wish
to see.
I'll ask no better. No? Now, pray, what better
can remain?
For there is not a single thought that I at all
disdain.

Yes, blessed, dear old treasure box, the bottom
part of twain;
And when I take it in my hand, I seldom take
in vain.

As if from some new fount of hope, where lasting
comforts flow,
My weary, care-worn soul is filled with ecstasy
below.

Now, who can sympathize with me in all that I
have said?
In truth, I do confirm the fact that heart and
box are wed.
From youth to happy maidenhood, and e'en as
age comes 'long,
It's been my love, my joy, my trust, my center,
and my song.

And while I tread the path of life, bestrewed with
toil and care,
The much that's good, the much that's ill, both
I expect to share;
But thou, like some kind, guardian friend, whose
faithful care doth keep,
Still treasureth up both new and old; why, there-
fore, do I weep?

OUR SOLDIER BOY.

OUR soldier boy is going,—
  How honorable the name,—
With a heart of rapture glowing
  For his country's glorious fame.
I saw upon his cheek no tear,
  No faltering voice was heard,
As round the family circle he
  Bespoke *that* farewell word.

Our soldier boy is going
  To face our country's foe,
With a stern and eager earnestness,
  His lot be weal or woe.
I saw, unveiled, his boy-like face,
  His gestures, new and old,
And wondered if great, gallant men
  Were even half as bold.

Our soldier boy is going,
His duty to fulfill,
With a hope of calm devotedness,
That 't is his Maker's will;
That, while the angry tempest
Is swelling in our land,
The high-throned God of battles
Will hold him in His hand.

Our soldier boy is going,—
We gave him freely up;
And if 't is He who calleth,
He'll sweeten every cup.
So if the shades of darkness
Are gath'ring o'er us now,
New springings forth of gladness
Will brighten every brow.

WAR'S DREADFUL SCOURGE.

WHY should we be thus deeply scourged?
Why is it that our country's merged
In such a scene of heart-felt woe
Beyond description? Dreadful blow!

How many dear, loved circles broke;
How many farewell words been spoke!
Then part, perhaps to meet no more
Again till all life's comfort's o'er.

'T is hard, 't is truly hard to know
That we should feel this scourging blow,
This contest deep, this frigid gale,
These base, uncomely acts assail.

When onward to the seat of woe
We let our own imag'nings go,

We see, as through a telescope,
The harshness of the cruel stroke.

We see, or think we see, the hosts
There marshaled to their inland posts,
With all the weapons to arrest
And quell the enemy abreast;

To wound and kill, to brave and take,
According as their strength can make.
And so the parties, two and two,
Fight on, and push the conquest through.

Have done, and done,—are doing still,
Till hundreds felt the deadly chill;
For from their wounds the life-blood rose
Till each and every vital froze.

While others, stiffened, mangled, lay,
Perchance unheeded for a day;
No promise bright, no prospect clear,
No welcome home, no friend to cheer,

But on a low, rough couch of earth,
Best pillow the down-trodden turf,
These weary, careworn sufferers lay,—
Amid the fires of battle pray.

What suffering! Can we paint too bold?
Methinks could never half be told;
For who 'mong mortals can express
The anguish of such dire distress?

I would this war could have an end,
Ere many more their lives should spend;
And love and peace triumphant reign
In our once happy land again.

PEACE, NOT WAR.

Friends and freemen, let us pity
  And for our country pray,
That this foul and fiendish slaughter
  Ere long may pass away;
That the sun which seems so clouded
  May break into our fold,
And the light of peace, so pleasant,
  We may again behold.

Heavenly Father, wilt thou hear us
  From yonder highland throne,
And spread thy banners over us
  As e'er before hath known?
We do need Thee in the nation,—
  Inspire the ruler's heart,
That soon by our ruler's judgment
  This error may depart.

When we think how many hundreds
  And thousands in the field,
With a poor and scanty ration,
  Thus subjugated yield,
It does send a thrill of sorrow
  Into the secret soul,
Pangs of the deepest horror, such
  That we can scarce control.

Let us tell it, let us talk it,
  From every hillside bend,
Until every heartless foeman
  Becomes a heart-felt friend.
And let not a transient spirit
  Attempt to make us twain,
But to bind us nearer, dearer,
  To life, to live again.

THE DECEASED SOLDIER.

The following refers to a friend who enlisted as a soldier in behalf of his country August 2d, 1862, was wounded at Gettysburg, recovered, and again became established where he remained a true and faithful helper until arrested by disease, which terminated his mortal course, August 6th, 1864.

He manly left his native home,
  In vigor and in pride,
His bible, blanket, knapsack, all,
  And musket at his side.

His seeing eye with tears o'er flowed;
  His heart ne'er faltered yet,
And, with the gloom that hovered round,
  He knew no word, regret.

He eagerly pursued his way,
  Regarding each behest,
Till brigadier, and comrades all,
  And each one loved him best.

His ready place he always knew,
  Until at length he fell,
Upon a day in battle fray,
  Amid the shot and shell;

But not to die. Upreared again,
  Once more he took his stand,
A warrior true and strenuous,
  To sway the rebel band.

And well he played the soldier's part,
  Though strange it seemed to me
That he was classed among the sons
  Who fought for liberty.

Not that I thought him less than all,
  Or torpid in his might;
But mem'ry of those by-gone days
  Came fresh as yesternight.

I knew him when a barefoot boy,
  With roguish plans on hand;
And many a time my eye has traced
  His footprints in the sand.

How little thought what time would bring,
  Or e'er that foot would tread
Upon the battle-field, among
  The dying and the dead.

But so it's been; yet, thankful we
  To Him who rules on high,
Though marshaled to an inland field,
  There was not doomed to die.

But by disease was swept away,
  Close lulled in death's embrace;
No more to give the friendly hand,
  Or fill a warrior's place.

Yes, gone beyond the battle ground,
  From 'mong the rebel throng,—
Where kindred meet in friendship sweet,
  The vigilant and strong.

Though tears may fall, and speech bewail,
  And time seem long and drear,
He 'll still sleep on, that lasting sleep,
  That knows no wak'ning here.

THE WAR FIEND.

A WEARY watchword on the wind,
  A blast too rudely blows
An angry tempest in our land,
  And bleeding hearts o'erflows,
Not only there amid the throng
  That's gathered in the field,
With nothing nearer than the heav'ns,—
  The starry heav'ns that shield,—
Is sadly felt this chilling blast,
  This tempest, fierce and wild;
But nearest, dearest, tendrils break,—
  The mother and the child.

Could we but trace where thousands trod,
  O'er mount and craggy dell,
Or span the rivers deep and wide,
  And their low murmurings tell,

Tell how has swept, is sweeping still,
  And hurrying away,
The dear and loveliest of our youth,
  The sparkling and the gay,
It then would ope this tragic scene
  Of infamy in store,
Into the heart and soul of man
  As never ope'd before.

'T is such a sad, tremendous thing,—
  This horrid form of war,—
That man by man so cruelly
  Be laid in drenching gore
Upon a field beneath the rays
  Of most resplendent light,
Their bodies shivered, tattered, torn,
  Amid an angry fight.
Could ever God or angels stoop,
  With condescending smile,
Upon a nation so enraged,
  A nation so revile?

Methinks we never can expect
  Promotion from on high,

Until the error of our race
  Is left to droop and die.
Let human wisdom, then, direct,—
  Humanity prevail;
The angry tempest then will sink
  Into a peaceful gale.
No more need sentinels be placed,
  No more the cannon roar;
No more need suffering sons of men
  Lie drenching in their gore.

FAREWELL.

"THERE are those upon whose ear the harsh word Farewell never breaks."

BENEATH, O heavens, thy starry throne,
  On some fair inland plain,
Where oft is heard the joyous bird,
  And love lights not in vain;
Where scepters of a golden hue
  Are borne with stately pride,
Where man rejoices with himself,
  His bonny and his bride;
Think ye that there the farewell word
  Breaks not upon the ear?
The whistling winds from woodland groves,
  Answer: Here,—it is here.

Is there no province in the east,
  No parish far away,
Where friendship, love, and happiness
  Bear one fraternal sway?
Where kindness, truth, and grace are borne
  As on an eagle's wing,
And plant within the human heart
  The offering that they bring?
Think ye that there the farewell word
  Could break upon the ear?
List, and a sound from the low brooks would
  Answer: Here,—it is here.

Could it be in that temperate zone
  Where, we've so oft been told
That brooks and running rivers have
  Those precious sands of gold?
That the glittering ore lies buried deep,
  'Neath flowing tide the price,
Beside which many a miner's built
  His fire of sacrifice?
Think ye that there the farewell word
  Ne'er breaks upon the ear?
List, and an echo from a thousand hills
  Answers: Here,—it is here.

It cannot be within our State,
  Where rude default is found,
Where bravely tread our gallant troops
  Upon the blood-washed ground;
Or where the gray-haired sires sit
  Beneath their weight of pain,
Bemoaning that their loved and lost
  Can ne'er come back again.
Think ye that here the farewell word
  Breaks not upon the ear?
List, for a voice like thunder from each State
  Answers: Here,—it is here.

It must be, then, beyond this world,
  Where joy's a fleeting boon,
In that delightful hemisphere
  Of unbeclouded noon
Where happy spirits dwell with God,
  And things celestial seen,
Where waves the tree, the tree of life,
  Of life, in living green.
Think ye that there the farewell word
  Breaks not upon the ear?
Truly, a whisper from the uplifted clouds
  Answers: Here,—never here.

EPITAPHS.

A FAITHFUL wife, and mother kind,
Her family dear has left behind;
To yonder home has gone to meet
Kindred around the mercy-seat.

THOU, daughter dear, hast left us,
  In silence long to lay,
But we trust thy spirit's soaring
  In realms of brighter day.

AWAY to yonder lofty sphere
  The unbound soul hath flown;
On wings seraphic took its flight,
  To worship God alone.

THE fairest flowers of earth must fade;
 The noblest sure must die;
Earth has no sacred, hallowed boon,
 Or rest beneath the sky.
But transient moments, when have passed,
Bring life, unchanging life at last.

HIS body, embalmed and in soldier's garb,
 It was tenderly born to the tomb.
We mourn, though his hope of salvation thro' Christ
 Expels the dark shadows of gloom.

Now every care has passed and gone,
 No thoughts involve the breast,
But in thy silent hiding-place
 Thou 'lt sleep and be at rest.
Our Maker's eye attends the spot,
Nor wilt thou ever be forgot.

www.ingramcontent.com/pod-product-compliance
Lightning Source LLC
LaVergne TN
LVHW011208110826
845150LV00006B/1365

9781425518103